The Solstice E

History, Folklore and Origins of the Christmas Tree

by
Sheryl Karas

Aslan Publishing
P.O. Box 108
Lower Lake, CA 95457
(707) 995-1861

Published by

Aslan Publishing
P.O. Box 108
Lower Lake, CA 95457
(707) 995-1861
For a free catalog of our other titles,
or to order more copies of this book
please call (800) 275-2606

Library of Congress Cataloging-in-Publication Data:

Karas, Sheryl, 1958-
    The solstice evergreen : history, folklore, and origins of the
Christmas tree / by Sheryl Karas. -- 1st ed.
        p. cm.
    Includes bibliographical reference and index.
    ISBN 0-944031-26-9 : $10.95
    1. Christmas trees. I. Title.
GT4989.K37 1991
398.2'88282--dc20

                                           90-1168
                                            CIP
                                            AC

The illustrations entitled: "Nude Woman with the Zodiac" on pg. 51, "The Virgin in Glory" on pg. 70, "Expulsion from Paradise" on pg. 11, and "The Fall" on pg. 11 are by Albrecht Dürer and reprinted from *The Complete Woodcuts of Albrecht Dürer,* edited by Dr. Willi Kurth, copyright 1963 by permission of Dover Publications, Inc.
Illustration on pg. 50 of Navajo Sand Painting is reprinted from *American Indian Design & Decoration* by Leroy H. Appleton by permission of Dover Publications, Inc., 1971.
Illustration on pg. 18 Cranach, "The Golden Age," Munich. Alte Pinakothek, used by permission of Giraudon/Art Resource
Illustration on pg. 100 Giovanni da Modena, "Redemption from the Fall of Man," Bologna, S. Peronio, used by permission of Alinari/Art Resource.
Illustration on pg. 57 Bosch, "Garden of Earthly Delights," Prado, used by permission of Marburg/Art Resource.
Illustration on pg. 73 Rubens, "Venus and Adonis," and pg. 77 "Roman Sarcophagus," used by permission of The Metroopolitan Museum of Art, NY.
Copyright free illustrations used throughout from *Traditional Chinese Designs* by Stanley Appelbaum © 1987, Dover; *Pictorial Archive of Decorative Renaissance Woodcuts* by Jost Amman © 1968, Dover; *Picture Book of Devils, Demons and Witchcraft* by Ernst andJohanna Lehner © 1971, Dover; *An Old Fashioned Christmas in Illustration & Decoration* by Clarence Horning © 1975, Dover; *Pictorial Archive of Decorative Frames & Labels* ed. by Carol Belanger Grafton © 1982, Dover; *The Plant Kingdom Compendium* ed. by Jim Harter © 1988, Bonanza Books, NY.
Photo of rug on pg. 48 by Covello & Covello Photography, Santa Cruz, CA.

Cover illustration by Sheryl Karas
Cover and book design by Brenda Plowman
Printed in USA
First Edition

10 9 8 7 6 5 4

To John,
whose enthusiasm and determination
to pursue the things he loves is a constant source
of joy and inspiration.

ACKNOWLEDGMENTS

Does anyone else love to read the acknowledgments and dedications at the front of books? I like to get glimpses of what goes into the creative process. This book was a very personal project, but without the help and support of dozens of people it would not exist. I am truly grateful for their efforts.

First, I would like to thank Dawson Church at Aslan Publishing for providing me with the motivation to finish this project that had been set aside for more than four years. I especially appreciate his thoughtful editing and suggestions on how to reorganize my work to the end I envisioned. It was a very cooperative process.

The research for this book was done primarily in libraries. One thing I learned was that librarians do a lot more than check out and reshelve books. Thank-you to the librarians at the Boston and Cambridge Public libraries, the Tozzer Library at Harvard University's Peabody Museum, and the Library of Congress in Washington D.C. for their assistance.

In addition to my husband, I wish to thank Jim Coleman and Bill Muench for bringing me into the computer age on two different systems. Their technical assistance turned a large box full of notebooks, index cards and odd pieces of paper into an easy-to-manage 3 1/2- inch disk. It's a pleasure to be past the point of yelling at incomprehensible machines to find myself actually enjoying their use.

I am especially indebted to my family, housemates and friends in New England for reading and honestly commenting on my manuscript early in its development. Several of their comments were instrumental in turning what could have been a dry academic thesis into a book everyone could enjoy. Their enthusiasm and support helped sustain this project during the times it seemed too overwhelming.

Likewise, I am indebted to my new friends and counselors in Santa Cruz, CA. It was their unflagging confidence and encouragement to talk about my work that helped me to push ahead despite feelings of being stuck and defeated. They knew I could do it, and here's the book to prove it!

Finally, I've reserved a special thank-you for my husband, John Rible. His support of me goes far beyond the realm of spousal duty. The many ways he shows his love for me have literally changed my life. It's almost a cliche for authors to thank their spouses in dedications and acknowledgments, but there really is no other support that matters more.

CONTENTS

Throughout this presentation of the origins and development of the Christmas Tree, I focus on folklore which illustrates the sacred significance of the tree. Although folklore is often neglected in historical studies of cultural phenomena, no other medium can so colorfully and accurately portray the daily life, beliefs and attitudes of a particular society.

There are, of course, drawbacks to this approach. Most myths, legends and fairy tales were passed orally from one generation to the next by storytellers whose use of dramatization and inflection added meaning that cannot be captured adequately on paper. Written versions of the stories have sometimes been changed beyond recognition by authors who omit or add according to their own beliefs. Priests, who were often the only literate people in many societies, were especially prone to slant myths and stories to emphasize their own priorities. This is seen most clearly in missionaries' versions of Native American tales.

A raging debate continues among modern storytellers. Should a tale be told exactly as it was found? Is it a form of sacrilege to update a fairy story? Despite past abuses, I think not. It can be assumed that the most "authentic" story was changed and updated many times before it was ever put on paper. Over time and travel the stories changed to fit the mores of the era. The tales constantly varied, merged and blended — their fluidity is frozen when put on paper and treated as literature. Instead of a living art form they risk becoming "dead," period pieces so obviously anachronistic as to have outlived their usefulness except from an historical perspective. Yet they are only mirrors of the times in which they were recorded. Until then the stories had a life of their own, which was not confined to a particular time in history.

No serious attempt to find "the most authentic version" of the tales included has been made here. I have taken the liberty of presenting the stories as if I were the storyteller, trying to keep the basics as close to whatever versions I found as possible. If I found more than one version of a story I chose the one I liked the best or wrote a composite of all of them.

I have made two exceptions. "The Juniper Tree" as recorded by the Brothers Grimm

1

has been treated as a piece of written literature for so long that I thought it best to leave it alone.

I also have not made changes in "The Fir Tree" by Hans Christian Andersen. Recognizing that all stories were originally made up by somebody, I decided it was proper to include a fairy tale by Andersen, a known author. Andersen told his tales out loud, like all true storytellers, but since he also wrote them down and signed his name to them, they do not quite fit the genre of an orally transmitted tale. Still, it seemed a fitting story with which to end this book.

Growing up Jewish in a typically Christian New England town made the Christmas season a confusing and lonely time of year for me. I remember making paper chains and other tree ornaments during art period in the first or second grade. After excitedly running home with my treasures I was stunned to face my parents' outrage that "Christianity" was being preached in the public schools. Later, when my glee club practiced for our annual Christmas-time recital I struggled with guilt for singing gentile songs. Yet, in calmer moments, I secretly wondered about the mysterious night of silver bells, herald angels, the star and, of course, Santa Claus and the flying reindeer.

Swept up by school activities, television programming and my friends' excitement each year as December 25th approached, I could feel my own anticipation building. Maybe THIS YEAR would be different. But once again, when the day arrived, there was nothing special about it. It was just a day like any other except I knew that everyone else was doing something wonderful—or so it seemed.

My mother did her best to offset the yearly cultural onslaught. Chanukah became a more important holiday than it was before. Family activities, outings to the movies, and imaginative Chanukah decorations served to make the season more bearable. Eventually I stopped looking forward to Christmas but I never stopped feeling somewhat sad when the day arrived. In later years we started to exchange presents at Chanukah, but that did not help; the real problem was hard to define. I did not feel drawn by the story of the Nativity. Neither did I feel the absence of a feast, with special foods and lots of family present, since we had occasions like that throughout the year. What I yearned for was the magic, the specialness of the day. And the most magical thing of all for me was the Christmas Tree.

As an adult my fascination with the tree stayed with me. When I was twenty-two my housemates and I bought a small pine to decorate our apartment and I enjoyed having a Christmas Tree in my own home for the first time. We dressed it with garlands of strung popcorn and cranberries, various homemade and sentimental ornaments, lots of tinsel and tiny colored lights. It was a bittersweet occasion. Voices from the past tried to convince me to feel guilty about participating in a Christian ritual, but the warmth I shared with my friends as we set up the tree and exchanged gifts and stories around it remains a cherished memory.

Later that evening, while cleaning my glasses, I happened to glance up at the tree. Looking at it through nearsighted eyes caused rays of light from the ornaments and glittering tinsel to fill the entire corner of the room. The tree was transformed into a shimmering vision of pure color and light.

The effect this had on me was similar to that of a spectacular sunset. I could sit forever watching the play of colors on the clouds change in intensity and hue as the sun sinks lower in the sky. I like to see how the world, especially grass and trees, increases in clarity as shadows deepen and the light still glows.

I sat with the tree the same way, utterly transfixed by its beauty. I felt as delighted as a child, relaxed and at peace. An hour passed before I had gotten my fill of looking at it.

Ever since that evening the Christmas Tree has been an integral part of my winter celebration. However, because of my background, I needed to clarify the meaning of the tree in my life before I could feel completely comfortable with this new ritual. In this process I began to wonder about the significance of the custom in our culture as a whole.

Many people are aware that the Christmas Tree is a vestige of the ancient religious practice of using evergreens to symbolize life in the dead of winter. They may have heard it was a "quaint" custom incorporated into the observance of Christmas by the Roman Catholic Church to appease the superstitions of the newly converted. Yet these simple explanations of the origin of the tree do not answer the question. Why was the sanctity of the evergreen so important to the newly Christianized masses that this tradition needed to be kept when many other aspects of paganism were neglected or destroyed? Neither does it explain the continuing popularity of the tree today even among people who reject most traditions and religious practices.

When I went to the local library and bookstores I found surprisingly little on the subject. Surely I was not the only person who wondered about the pre-Christian origin of the Christmas Tree? Eventually I found a variety of Christmas folk stories which led me to investigate my subject through the realm of folklore rather than conventional history.

The evergreen played an influential role in the spiritual life of early societies throughout the world. Archaeological and anthropological evidence indicates that veneration of the tree dates from at least 4000 years before Christ. Its pervasive symbolism was central to primitive cosmologies, the beliefs about the universe which laid the foundation for every major religion, including Christianity. These pagan beliefs survive to this day embedded in religious rituals and myths as well as in secular customs, legends and fairy tales.

After a brief introduction to early religion and mythology, this book traces the roots of the Christmas Tree through the ancient symbolism and mythology of the evergreen. It discusses how these beliefs became so widespread and deeply entrenched, and concludes with a brief history of the Christmas Tree from the time of Christ to the present day.

Because the subject of evergreens is so broad I have limited the book to the discussion of evergreens which might be used for a Christmas Tree. This includes all species of pine and fir, spruce, cedar and cypress. Myths, legends and fairy tales about these trees and the Christmas Tree, are scattered throughout the text to illustrate the key points introduced in each chapter.

Many people like to de-emphasize our pagan heritage. We have been taught to associate paganism with violent practices and, therefore, find it threatening to see pagan aspects in our modern "civilized" religions. Yet paganism is much more than human sacrifice. It is part of our spiritual past. In the case of the Christmas Tree, this knowledge can enrich the celebration of the ritual for even the most fundamentalist Christians and revitalize the winter holidays for those who are not.

"Gathering Christmas Greens." An illustration from c. 1876.

CHAPTER ONE

The Nature of Religion– the Religion of Nature

Everything that lives is holy.
—William Blake, THE MARRIAGE OF HEAVEN AND HELL

*Thou, nature, art my goddess; to thy law
my services are bound.*
—William Shakespeare, KING LEAR

It was fear that first brought gods into the world.
—Petronius Arbiter, SATYRICON

Every year at Christmas time, otherwise rational, conventional, serious-minded adults participate in an unusual ritual. A special time is set aside for a pilgrimage to the forest or corner Christmas Tree lot where after a great deal of deliberation and discussion the "perfect" evergreen tree is selected. It is brought home and set up in a place of honor in the main common room in the house. Then boxes of decorations for the tree are retrieved from where they have been carefully stored during the previous year. New decorations are lovingly made or thoughtfully selected and bought.

Every family has its special ornaments— the lopsided angel made by a now-grown child, the crystal baubles handed down from one generation to the next. Some families have color schemes and fancy store-bought trimmings. Others choose homemade ornaments made of paper and glitter, styrofoam balls covered with ribbons and beads, and macrame snowflakes stiffened with glue. There are edible decorations—candy canes, baskets of chocolates, sugar cookies and sugarplums. There are even people who set up a tree for their animals or birds covered with foods these creatures like to eat—carrots and apples, seeds, popcorn, even dog biscuits.

When the tree is completely dressed, a star or an angel is placed at the top, presents are piled underneath and the string of electrical lights usually draped around its branches is plugged in. Someone almost invariably turns the house lights down, and the family gathers around to admire their handiwork.

Throughout the Christmas season celebrations include the tree as a centerpiece. Carols are sung around it. Gifts are exchanged beneath it. Christmas dinner guests take special care to compliment the hosts on its beauty. Nobody claims to worship the tree, but if a visitor from another planet interpreted these rituals in such a way it would hardly be surprising.

Why else would anyone do something so strange, so whimsical, and so special? Many people say they do it for the sake of their children. They like to see their children's eyes light up, or they hope to impress upon them the specialness of the season. Yet childless adults are equally likely to set up a tree.

Perhaps the tree is for the child in each of us. It reminds us of when we looked at the world through younger eyes—the time when everything we saw was wondrous and worthy of our closest attention. It was also a time when we believed in infinite possibilities, and the fairy tales we were read at night were not just an escape from the everyday world but a promise of the magic and power a life lived well might provide.

In a world so thoroughly dominated by science and rationality, the Christmas Tree stands out as evidence of the side of our nature that is drawn to fairy tales—the side that deals with myth and symbol. To understand the significance of the evergreen tree it is essential to start with an understanding of how myths operate in our lives.

Myth-Directed Lifestyle

Today the word "myth" is often used as a synonym for "misconception" or "lie." However, the historical accuracy of myths may have been unimportant. They were, and are, simply stories—which symbolically illustrate a set of action-guiding beliefs.

To varying degrees, we all live according to the myths we were taught as children. Even when we reject religious or societal myths we are still guided by self-made ones. We grow up believing we are intelligent or dim-witted, artistic or uncreative, athletic or clumsy and can recite the appropriate stories from our past to justify our present-day beliefs and actions. An example of using myths in a more conscious manner can be found among techniques which harness the power of positive thinking.

One such technique involves remembering and telling the stories of times one was successful at solving a problem similar to a problem one is encountering in the present. If no such story is available then one visualizes a positive outcome to the present situation and tells that story. The idea is to use these stories to contradict the impulse to focus on negative past experiences. This frees the person's attention to focus on the present. It helps one to release the painful emotions from the past that prevent flexible thinking, and it facilitates decisive action.

When one lives as if the positive stories are reflections of what is really possible the chances of reaching success greatly increase. This is because people who believe they can be successful behave differently from those who think they will fail. They make the myths reality.

Religious myths work the same way. The ancient tales were created to teach the rules of the universe, as they were then understood, and the best ways to live according to those rules. The ideas and values so imparted shaped whole civilizations, keeping them stable as each generation grew up under their guidance.

When a new religion with its attendant mythology was introduced to a community through casual contact with other peoples, compatible aspects of the strangers' religion were absorbed. Other aspects were modified to fit the society's needs or simply rejected. However, when a new religion was aggressively infused it threatened not only the continuity of the existing religious tradition but also the basis for the community's structure and way of life.

Lifestyle-Directed Religion

Our modern civilizations have changed so drastically from the cultures which produced the ancient stories it is sometimes hard to identify the deep truths embedded in these highly imaginative tales. Since they were usually elaborations of common experiences, the task of interpreting the symbolism becomes easier when seen in the light of how early people lived.

Christianized Western Caucasian civilization considers the human being a superior creature, and glorifies attempts to rise above or control nature. This outlook would be almost inconceivable to most primal peoples.

Our ancestors lived in a world in which the natural environment was the only environment. They knew that survival was based on noticing and respecting the interdependence of everything around them and never questioned their own place in the cosmic order. Early people felt that the whole world was alive and imbued with consciousness, emotion and intelligence resembling their own. Therefore, they treated entities in their environment with the same respect they would show another human being. Their assumption of the unity of a living world was the basis for most religions.

At some point people started to wonder what caused living things to die. What did a living person have that a dead one did not have? Through the experience of dreams and other phenomena the idea developed that individuals had a soul or spirit which left the body at death. Naturally, since humans were just one part of a living world, this concept was extended to animals, trees, plants and everything else in the universe. Social scientists call this belief animism.

Over a period of 20,000 years, prehistoric people slowly started to change their environments. They developed their own languages and tribal societies, learned to make tools and clothing, and, by 9000 B.C., were starting to farm. Since these were activities unique to humankind, people began to see themselves as different. In gaining the ability to think about and change their surroundings they had begun to lose their instinctual feeling about their place in nature. As time went on, and people depended more on their societies and technology, it became possible to survive without an intimate knowledge of the workings of nature. As a result, the world outside of the one they could control became increasingly less familiar and more forbidding.

This period in the development of civilization is symbolized by the story of Adam and Eve. As recounted in the Book of Genesis, Adam and Eve lived harmoniously with all creatures in the Garden of Eden until they ate from the forbidden Tree of Knowledge. It was then that they first noticed they were naked—they became aware of themselves separate from their environment. Consequently banished from the Garden they were doomed to live lives of toil and suffering—they lived by the fruits of their labor rather than by gathering the fruits of their environment. They were prevented from returning to their previously safe home by a fearsome angel with a fiery sword. The natural world, as symbolized by the Garden, became a beloved yet frightening place.

In order to gain more control over nature early people turned to the use of magic. If an object had a spirit like a person did—or so the idea went—then perhaps it could be persuaded to make certain events happen, in the

same way a person could be persuaded. Prayers and gifts were offered to whatever entity a particular tribe felt was most powerful. At this time magic was an expression of individual or group power. Because most members of a tribe were busy with other survival-oriented tasks, the creation of necessary ceremonies and spells was left to one person, the shaman, or a small group of people who specialized in using this power.

The First Roots ceremony once performed by the Flathead tribe in Montana is a good example of the use of powerful rituals. This ceremony was performed early in the spring before the women were allowed to start the seasonal gathering of roots, a staple of the Flathead diet. Two older women would lead a small group of women to a favorite gathering place. The oldest then prayed to the sun for success, security, good health and fortune for her tribe. She then addressed the earth, asking for the same blessings. The group dug up a small supply of roots and brought them back to camp where they were used in a ritual meal. The food thus prepared symbolized all the food they would gather that season. Before it was eaten it was blessed again by prayers to the sun and earth.

At some point the concept of spirits as differentiated from the objects they inhabited arose. Some societies believed that when someone or something died its soul could transmigrate into something else. For example, the Chinese once believed the spirits of their ancestors lived in certain trees or other objects. Rituals which had been performed for the "living corn plant" were then done for the "spirit who lives in corn." People believed the increasing or decreasing strength of the spirits made the seasons change, and events in the lives of the spirits affected the lives of everyone.

Although at first tribes or their shamans felt their own powerful spirits and magic could be enough to persuade other spirits to do their bidding, over time, they came to depend less on their own power and more on the mediation of stronger deities. This was the time of polytheism, the belief in many gods and goddesses. A few thousand more years passed before the desire for all-powerful divine benefactors and the age-old knowledge of cosmic unity evolved into the monotheistic religions we know today.

Why Some Trees Are Evergreen

Cherokee tribe, North America

When the plants and trees were first made the Great Mystery gave a gift to each species. But first he set up a contest to determine which gift would be most useful to whom.

"I want you to stay awake and keep watch over the earth for seven nights," he told them.

The young trees and plants were so excited to be trusted with such an important job that the first night they would have found it difficult not to stay awake. However, the second night was not so easy, and just before dawn a few fell asleep. On the third night the trees and plants whispered among themselves in the wind trying to keep from dropping off, but it was too much work for some of them. Even more fell asleep on the fourth night.

By the time the seventh night came the only trees and plants still awake were the cedar, the pine, the spruce, the fir, the holly and the laurel.

"What wonderful endurance you have!" exclaimed the Great Mystery. "You shall be given the gift of remaining green forever. You will be the guardians of the forest. Even in the seeming dead of winter your brother and sister creatures will find life protected in your branches."

Ever since then all the other trees and plants lose their leaves and sleep all winter while the evergreens stay awake.

The Two Pine Cones

Finland

A Laplander wizard, who was on a journey through Finland, arrived at a town early one evening hungry and bone-weary. Oh, how he wished he could spend the night in a warm inn, but with no money his only choices were to find a protected spot outside or beg for a place to sleep.

On the edge of town there was a small hut made of logs. It would have been so nice to be able to stop walking right there, but the wizard passed by, thinking, "These people have so little themselves. If I go to a larger home the people will be more able to help me."

The next house looked promising, large and well-kept, obviously the home of well-to-do folk. He knocked on the door but at first there was no answer. He tried again and a cold harsh voice called out, "Who are you? And what business do you have knocking on decent folk's doors at this hour?"

The wizard answered, "Pardon me. I am but a poor wayfarer who needs a place to rest his head. Would you allow me a corner by your stove for the night?"

The woman answered, "Go away! I have no room for beggars. Move on or I'll set loose the dogs."

The wizard returned to the poor hut where he was welcomed in by a kind-looking woman and her husband. They shared their small evening meal with him and, at bedtime, gave him their only bed.

In the morning the wizard wished to repay them by giving the woman the ring he wore on his finger, but she said no, she couldn't take it. The wizard then drew a pine cone from his cloak. "Take this then instead. It will help you prosper in the first task you do today."

The woman took the pine cone and thanked him. Then she turned to her work. Her first job was to measure the linen she had woven the day before. She measured and measured but, to her surprise, the more she measured the more there was. It took her three days to measure it all. By that time there was enough linen to last her family for the rest of their lives.

The story of the poor woman's good fortune was told throughout the village. Her rich neighbor fretted about her lost opportunity and decided she would treat the stranger differently if he ever came back.

A year passed by, and sure enough, the wizard did pass through town again. He stopped again at the big house and this time was ushered in with a smile. The woman of the house prepared a feast of the finest foods and gave him the finest feather bed to sleep on.

In the morning the wizard wished to pay her for her kindness but she refused his money. He drew a pine cone from his cloak as he had done before. He said, "Take this then instead. It will help you prosper in the first task you do today."

The greedy woman was looking forward to this moment and had set a purse of gold on her table all ready to count. But in her excitement she sneezed before she reached the table and without thinking ran to get a handkerchief.

To her horror she found herself unable to do anything but sneeze, run for her handkerchief, sneeze and run, sneeze and run again. It took three days before she could stop sneezing long enough to put away her purse.

When Your Canary Sings

Hartz Mountains, Germany

Once upon a time, on a Christmas Eve, a fierce winter storm raged through the Hartz Mountains. Heavy with sleet and snow, the wind howled and whirled violently—with such force it splintered even the mightiest trees and sent them crashing to the valley below. The only ones who could withstand the terrible temper of the north wind were the old majestic firs, who held on steadfastly with their gnarled roots.

In occasional brief lulls the fir trees could hear the frightened cries of tiny golden canaries who were being flung to and fro in the powerful wind. "Ohhh! Ohhh! We're going to die! How can we get out of this storm?"

The trees called into the wind knowing it would bring their message to the birds. "Come to us! We will protect you in our branches."

The exhausted canaries, using their last reserves of strength, flew into the arms of the giant firs, where they stayed safely until the storm was over. When at last the world was quiet and the sun peeked out from behind the last remaining clouds, the birds burst out into joyous song. "We will make our homes with you and sing our praises to you forever wherever we go. You shall be the sacred home of birds all over the world."

So now when your canary is singing his sweetest you know he is singing about the wonderful fir tree.

Pitys and Boreas

Greece

There once was a nymph named Pitys whose duty it was to tend pine trees. Her lover was Boreas, god of the north wind. She loved his strong blustery nature but was also attracted to the more carefree god Pan so flirted with them both.

One day Boreas asked Pitys what was going on between her and Pan, but she was too frightened to give him a direct answer. Boreas lost his temper in the quarrel that followed and threw Pitys against a rocky ledge where she was instantly turned into a pine tree. The resin droplets seen on wounded limbs of pine trees broken by the north wind are the teardrops shed by Pitys.

"The Golden Age," by Lucas Cranach the Elder.

CHAPTER TWO

Sacred Trees and Groves

Among the scenes which are deeply impressed on my mind,
none exceed in sublimity the primeval forests
undefaced by the hand of man.
No one can stand in these solitudes unmoved,
and not feel that there is more in man
than the mere breath of his body.
—Charles Darwin

During the era just after the last ice age, Europe was covered with immense primeval forests. Germans questioned by Caesar claimed to have traveled for two months through the Hercynian forest eastward from the Rhine without ever reaching its end. It was said that a squirrel could cross all of England in the forest of Arden by jumping from one limb to the next.

Because prehistoric people depended on the forests for food and shelter, for fire, canoes, tools and household implements, trees were an important feature of their environment. Furthermore, they seemed to embody the cycle of Nature itself. They grew and made sounds, gave birth to flowers and fruit, "bled" when cut, became old and died. It is no wonder then that trees became special in the religious life of various societies both as representations of deities themselves, and as the sacred home of or place of communion with other spirits.

The most common deities found in mythologies worldwide were the Sun God, the Earth Mother and the Sky Spirit. These great spirits were considered so powerful that no temple was large enough or holy enough to contain them. There is a Latin saying, "Mundus universus est templum solis," which means "the whole world is a temple of the

sun." Accordingly, goddesses and gods were usually worshipped outdoors in naturally protected spots such as under the trees. Woods found or planted on hills and mountaintops were considered especially suitable places for holy observances. These sacred groves were the forbidden "high places" mentioned in the Old Testament.

Wherever sacred groves were established, they acted as sanctuaries, with the same significance as churches and temples hold for us today. People approached and entered them in reverent silence and with the utmost respect. It was sacrilegious and often dangerous to break branches or even pick a leaf. These groves sometimes also served as refuge for escaped prisoners. For example, a grove of cypress sacred to the Greek goddess Hebe was described by the ancient Greek writer Pausanias as decorated with the chains of prisoners who attained their freedom upon reaching it.

The Cedars of Lebanon

Probably the most famous sacred grove is the hilltop known as "the Cedars of Lebanon." Although the mountains in this area are today practically bare except for a stand of twelve giant cedars, they were once covered with a forest of these impressive trees. The Old Testament contains numerous references to the cedar. "The righteous shall grow like a cedar" proclaims one psalm. Another passage declares that "the trees of the Lord are full of sap, the cedars of Lebanon which he hath planted." The prophet Ezekiel compared Egypt to a fallen

cedar, a popular phrase indicating fallen glory.

Fallen cedars were a common sight in biblical days. After King Solomon convinced the Phoenicians to trade the cedars to build a temple in Jerusalem without incurring the wrath of the gods, the forest was ravaged by others for its timber. There would be no cedars left in the area today if the deeper value of the trees had not been insisted upon by various religious groups.

The Cedars of Lebanon are still called "arz el Rabb," the trees of the Lord. They are known to Israel as the Twelve Friends of Solomon, to Christians as the Twelve Apostles and to Mohammedans as the Saints. Every year at the Feast of the Transfiguration, hundreds of Armenians, Greeks and Muslims go on a pilgrimage to the area to worship and hear a mass. It is considered a sacrilege, as it was in pagan times, to injure the trees in any way.

Tree Spirits

The beliefs of aboriginal peoples offer an explanation for why trees and groves must not be hurt: Spirits live in the trees. If the tree is cut the spirit will die.

Tree spirits are known under a variety of different names—dryads, hamadryads, pixies, elves, genii, jinn, huldefolk, etc. They are sometimes described as green-skinned with mossy hair; other times they appear as extraordinarily small or large creatures with a human form. They are capable of mischief and hurt but are often regarded as friendly to those who respect them and the laws of nature. Tree spirits sometimes achieve the stature of gods and goddesses, but usually these beings can be thought of as personifications of the essence of nature.

In the northern countries of Europe pine trees are the favorite dwelling places of the forest spirit. He or she usually lives in a particularly old and gnarled pine, called the King of the Forest. Misfortune befalls anyone who should cut this tree down. The voice of the spirit is said to be heard in the rustle of leaves or in the murmur of the breeze.

In Finland, a tribe called the Votiaks recognize a tree spirit they call Nules-murt (Forest man). Nules-murt looks like a human being with only one eye stuck in the middle of its forehead. He is capable of changing size at will, sometimes appearing as a tiny elf, but usually standing as high as the tallest tree. He is sometimes called "Great Uncle" because of his height.

Nules-murt lives in the forest with his family, many treasures of gold and silver, and a large herd of cattle. He moves from place to place in a whirlwind and is enormously strong. Although he is said to lure away children and cattle, he is not feared or considered dangerous by the Votiaks. On the contrary, he is thought to be a special helper to good people, sending game to hunters and protecting them, their families and their cattle in the forest.

The Votiaks make offerings to the forest spirit in autumn under a great fir tree. All the hunters take part with offerings of brandy, bread, and a bull or a goat.

Ancient Tree Trimming

Worship around a tree is common worldwide. Even within the sacred groves, worship often centered around one special tree which may or may not have represented a higher deity. In either case it was usually larger than all the others or set apart in some other way.

Ceremonies honoring the tree involved sacrifices and holy offerings which were placed on the ground beneath it or in its branches. When the Spanish journeyed to the New World they found an ancient cypress in Mexico, revered by the Mayans, which had offerings of teeth and locks of hair attached to its boughs. In China sacred trees bore red banners with words of praise and thanksgiving painted on them in black. Greek and Roman goddesses and gods each had their special trees which were draped in cloth or garlands of flowers. Little masks of Bacchus called "oscilla" were also placed on the branches so they twirled freely in the wind. By honoring the popular agricultural god, the faces were supposed to encourage growth and fertility in whatever part of the tree they faced.

Another ritual in this vein, performed at the winter solstice, was recorded by early missionaries in Finland, who quickly modified the custom for the celebration of Christmas. Each year the Lapps collected a sampling of all the foods eaten at the solstice feast. These were put into a small birch bark trough shaped like a tiny sailing boat, complete with masts, sails and oars. The boat was placed in the branches of a special pine tree which was marked with sacred symbols on all four sides. They also slaughtered a reindeer and put offerings of the animal's internal organs in another pine, which was then smeared with reindeer blood.

The tree worship of the Druids in Europe is well known. Their special tree was the oak, but they also revered the fir, the rowan and the hazel. During the winter solstice they tied apples to the branches of oaks and firs to thank the god Odin for blessing them with fruitfulness. They also made offerings of cakes shaped like fish, birds and other animals. Lighted candles, honoring the sun god Balder, were placed in the boughs.

The connection between the Christmas Tree and the sacred tree is quite clear; however, if the tree were merely a representation of a powerful spirit, the early Christian church would probably have been successful in eliminating its celebration when the converts accepted the idea that the one god was supreme and the ancient gods were devils. The persistence of the tree makes it apparent that its symbolism was more important than the form of its worship.

Leelinau
Ojibway tribe, North America

When Leelinau was a young girl she loved to spend her time roaming quiet areas or sitting peacefully upon some high outcropping of rock overlooking a lake. Her favorite spot was a forest of pines called Manitowok or the Spirit Grove. This place on the open shore was not often visited by her people because it was said to be inhabited by mischievous fairy-like turtle-spirits. When people needed to pass through the wood or seek shelter within it, they always left an offering of tobacco for these keepers of the grove.

When Leelinau grew to marriageable age, her parents disapproved of her being away from home so much. One night they told her they had found a suitable man for her to marry. The young woman burst into tears. "I do not want to be married!" she sobbed.

That night she crept out of her parents' home and went to the Spirit Grove. She sat down against a young pine to decide what to do. She spent most of the evening, alternately crying and meditating, when finally she heard a voice come from the tree.

"Leelinau, I will be your lover," the pine tree said. "You may stay with me forever and find peace in my love and happiness in my protection. In my bark canoe, you will float over the waters of the sky-blue lake."

Leelinau's heart was flooded with relief and joy at these words. She returned home smiling and allowed her parents to continue with the wedding preparations. On the day she was to wed, she rose early and dressed in her wedding garments. She told her parents she wished to meet her lover at the Spirit Grove and they gave their consent. So Leelinau went into the forest and never came back.

Many moons later a group of fishermen spearing fish near the grove thought they saw Leelinau standing by the shore. They silently paddled toward land, but the young woman saw them and fled into the forest. She was never seen again.

Rata and the Children of Tane
Maori, New Zealand

In order to retrieve the bones of his murdered father, the hero Rata needed to travel to the Moonlight Land, far across the sea. His first step was to build a canoe. He went to his great-grandfather who gave him a beautiful greenstone axe. Then he strode into the Forest of Tane, the kauri forest, to find the perfect tree. The kauri are large cedars with trunks often a full one hundred feet long from ground to branches.

It took a while to find the best tree, one that was straight and tall enough to make the magnificent boat he imagined he needed for the difficult journey ahead. At last he found it and cut it down. By that time it was close to nightfall, so Rata went home to rest and prepare for a full day of boat-building.

In the night the children of Tane gathered, angry that the pride of the forest was gone. There were thousands of them—birds and insects of all sorts, wood-sprites and spirits. With their firm beaks and beating wings the birds managed to lift the fallen trunk while the insects and fairies collected every chip and grain of wood and set it back in place.

When Rata came the next morning the tree stood grandly, completely restored.

Rata sang an incantation to protect himself from evil and set to work again. When he had finished for the day the white-stripped outlines of a canoe lay nestled in the ferns.

With equal determination the forest children worked at night and by morning the tree stood tall and straight once more.

And so it happened again a third day and night. But on that last night Rata watched in secret. He saw the sky full of wings and the forest floor moving with birds and insects.

The spirits sang as they worked:
"Fly together chips and shavings,
Stick ye fast together,
Hold ye fast together;
Stand upright again, O tree!"

Rata stepped out from his hiding place and seized a fairy. "Why have you done this to my tree?" he demanded.

"Your tree, indeed" the fairy replied. "Who bestowed upon you the authority to enter the forest and cut down a beloved of Tane without permission?"

Then Rata felt ashamed that he had violated the sacred garden. He asked for forgiveness and told the spirits why he wanted the canoe.

The spirits agreed to help and told him to go home and return in the morning. When he returned he found a large and strongly-made canoe. It was so heavy, one hundred and forty warriors could not push it down to the water.

The spirits of the grove came to Rata's aid once more. They sent a message to the sky spirits. The sky spirits sent a rain that swelled a nearby river into a flood. The water rose higher and higher until it lifted the canoe and floated it down to the sea.

Rata and his warriors rowed away and met with great success.

The Pine of Akoya

Japan

Long ago, during the reign of Emperor Mommu, there lived a beautiful and talented woman named Akoya. Her father, Fujiwara Toyomitsu, was the governor of the province of Uzen. Akoya loved to play a stringed instrument called the koto, and the townspeople enjoyed its lovely sounds as they passed by her house.

One autumn evening as she sat playing alone, she heard a flute accompanying her sweetly and in perfect harmony. She shyly peeked out her door. There stood a handsome young man dressed in green. "My name is Natori Taro," he said. "I live at the foot of Mt. Chitose." The two fell deeply in love and spent many happy evenings with each other.

One night the man came to her filled with despair. "I am so sad. This is the last time I can visit you for my life will end tomorrow. I wish I did not have to say good-bye."

Then he disappeared and the shadow of a pine tree was seen on the sliding paper doors. Akoya was stunned and beside herself with worry.

It so happened that close to that time a bridge over the Natori River had been swept away by a flood. The next day construction of a new bridge was to begin, but lumber was in short supply. The villagers decided to cut down a big pine tree at the foot of Mt. Chitose. How could they have guessed that the spirit of the pine tree was the lover of the governor's daughter?

Woodcutters cut down the pine but when they tried to carry the tree to the Natori River, it could not be moved. Akoya heard of this and her lover's last words suddenly became clear. She rushed to the fallen pine and touched it lovingly. With tears in her eyes she pulled the rope with the other people. The tree miraculously lightened and the job was soon completed.

Akoya never married and lived alone the rest of her life. A young pine grew up in the place where the old one was cut down, and when that one died a new one took its place. To this day an old tree stands at the foot of Mt. Chitose in the suburbs of Yamagata-shi. It is called the Pine of Akoya.

The Shuralee and the Woodcutter
South Siberia, Soviet Union

One evening a woodcutter from Kurlai went into the forest to collect firewood. It was a beautiful quiet night and the man took his time in selecting a tree, walking quite deep into the woods. He at last came to a clearing where he spotted a good-sized spruce.

After settling his things down, he took out his axe and set to work. The rhythmic sound of the axe rang throughout the forest.

Suddenly there was a blood-curdling scream! Aighyeee! The woodsman jumped and spun around in terror. Right behind him stood a shuralee—a creature so grotesque that the man nearly fainted from the sight of it. It had a bony green face and a misshapen body with long thin arms and legs, all knotted and gnarled like the limbs of an old tree. It had a horn sticking out from the middle of its forehead and a fishhook for a nose. Its arms hung down half a yard with ten long sharp fingers.

The woodsman took a deep breath and stared into the shuralee's evil red eyes. "What do you want of me?" he asked with a tremble in his voice.

The shuralee shrieked and danced about. "You are a daring man, yes, you are, to come into my woods at night to cut one of my trees. I should tear you limb from limb. But have no fear. I won't do that. No, no! I will tickle you to death! I can scratch and tickle most wickedly with these fingers," it said as it waved and beckoned with each one for emphasis. "Come, my boy, and play a game of tickle with me, hee, hee, heeeeeeeeeeee!"

The woodcutter pretended to agree. "All right. But if I must pay for cutting this tree, at least let me finish the job. Help me fell it. Take hold here where I have cut a wedge, and when I shout, push!"

"Ah, ha, ha, ha, haaaa! Hee, hee, heeee! Why not?" The shuralee screeched and laughed as it put its awful fingers into the cut in the tree to take a firm grip. Just as he did the woodsman picked up the wedge his axe had cut from the tree and drove it back into the trunk, jamming the creature's fingers inside.

The shuralee shrieked and called the other forest demons to come to its aid. But none came.

It cowered and pleaded with the woodcutter to release him. "Take pity, take pity. Let me go. I promise I will not harm you. I will not harm you or your son. Or your son's son. Or any of your family or your descendants. I give you my word. Just let me go!"

The shuralee struggled, putting its hideous feet against the tree and pushing and pulling with all its might. It wailed like a siren and begged for mercy, but the woodcutter ignored it and prepared to go.

"Stop! Who are you, you heartless wretch? If I live to see another creature, who shall I say did this to me?"

"They call me Thistimelastyear." said the woodcutter. "Now I must be going."

The shuralee flung its body to and fro, screaming in its effort to escape and punish the man, but it could not free itself.

"Forest brothers! Demons! I summon you! I was trapped by Thistimelastyear. He left me to die, Thistimelastyear!"

Other shuralees did not run into the clearing until the next morning and, when they did, they showed no sympathy.

"Don't carry on so. You hurt our ears. If you got stuck this time last year why do you complain about it only now?"

Life for a Life
Germany

A malicious old woman once attempted to uproot the trunk of an ancient fir tree. In the midst of her labours she was suddenly struck by a frighteningly intense weakness. She was dizzy and scarcely able to walk. While trying to crawl home she met a mysterious stranger.

"Old woman," he said. "What is the matter with you?"

She told him her story and his face became very grave. "When you hurt the tree you hurt an elf who lives within it. If the elf recovers so will you. But if he should die, you will die as well."

The old woman made it home and went to bed with terror in her heart. She died that very night.

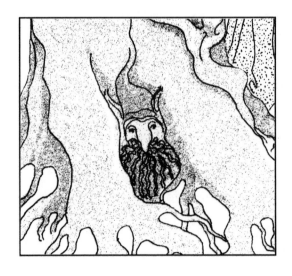

CHAPTER THREE

Evergreen Symbology

How strong, vital, enduring! How dumbly eloquent!
What suggestions of imperturbability and being,
as against the human trait of mere seeming.
Then the qualities, almost emotional, palpably artistic,
heroic, of a tree; so innocent and harmless, yet so savage.
—Walt Whitman, SPECIMEN DAYS

The Symbol

One wonderful skill human beings have is the ability to make analogies. We assess new objects and situations by comparing them to similar things we've encountered in the past. This is a highly effective survival technique, it being a matter of life or death to properly and quickly identify potentially dangerous objects and situations.

Through this process of analogy an everyday object can acquire connotations far beyond its obvious nature. Before writing was fully developed, people used a similar thought process to create pictures or visual symbols to convey information to others. For example, the symbol of the skull and crossbones is still used to label poisonous substances. Another symbol we all are familiar with is the heart, sign of love and affection. Even within language, symbols are used to represent abstract concepts that are not easily defined or understood. That is why most religions depend on symbols and parables to make spiritual messages clear.

Judaism teaches that God, the creator, is timeless and limitless, all-powerful, all-knowing and unknowable. In modern terms this definition might be construed to mean that God is a great creative life force or a collection of energies imbued with consciousness. Arab Moslems, who can trace their religion directly from Judaism, use the word "Allah," translated most accurately as "Essence," for God.

This concept of an invisible creative power which permeates every natural object in the universe is known to almost every culture. Sometimes it is split into many individual spirits who combine to make up the whole, as in primal and polytheistic cultures. Elsewhere it is thought to be one all-encompassing spirit as in Judaism, or one spirit with several forms, such as the Christian Trinity. Yet it is hard to imagine what an "essence" is, even though, with the widespread use of such words as "soul" or "spirit," it is obvious that most people believe in something similar to it. For that reason we create images that symbolize this power in terms that are more familiar.

Although I grew up with the teachings of Judaism and learned about the abstract nature of God at a young age, as a child, I visualized "Him" as a big old man with a long flowing white beard who lived in the clouds. And how could this man see everything and be everywhere at the same time? Why, he had a huge crystal ball like one the witch used in "The Wizard of Oz," of course.

I have discovered that this view of God is not unique among children, nor is it much different from the symbolism used in most religions. The Bible itself refers to God as "Him" and "He." Furthermore, can one truthfully imagine oneself praying to an essence? "Our Creative Life Force, Who art everywhere, Hallowed be Thy existence..." just does not have the comforting ring of "Our Father, Who art in Heaven, Hallowed be Thy name..." because it does not possess the same profound symbolism.

Chinese cranes in a pine tree

The Tree

As time goes on, usage makes the symbolism of an object almost inseparable from the object itself. This must be taken into account in any study of early religion. To say that primitives worshipped the trees, as many anthropologists assert, is to take the evidence too literally. To some extent it is true, yet rituals of the tree pay homage to more than the physical form or the spirit within it.

As an embodiment of nature the tree represented much of what gave meaning to everyday existence. Among other things it symbolized fertility and life, strength, and steadfastness of spirit. Where evergreens were abundant, they became the trees most highly revered, because while other trees lost their leaves and seemed to die or at least fall asleep during the winter, the evergreens stayed fresh and green through the most severe weather. This seemed to be proof of their extra power. In addition to the qualities embodied by other trees, they came to symbolize eternal life, the promise that life would continue forever.

Because of this strong symbolism, the Chinese god of longevity was often portrayed as sitting under a pine tree with a crane, another longevity symbol, perching in its branches. It was the custom in China to plant cypress or pine trees on the graves of loved ones, so the souls of the deceased could gain strength from the tree, or perhaps live on within it, and the body be preserved from decay. People who wished to live longer drank tea made from boiled pine needles and cones or from the fungus found at the roots of pines. The older the tree from which these medicines were collected, the stronger the magical effect. The pine also symbolized friendship in the face of adver-

Cypress trees are planted in graveyards as a symbol of eternal life.

sity. Many Chinese and Japanese legends tell of lovers whose spirits dwelt in the same pine, or in entwined pine trees, after death.

This legend is also known in Europe. Celtic mythology speaks of the couple Naisi and Deirdre. Yew stakes were driven through their bodies to keep them apart, but after they died they became yew trees. The tops of the two trees are said to embrace over Armagh Cathedral. Another Celtic legend tells the story of Cyperissa from whose grave grew the first cypress. This story is reminiscent of the Greek myth about Cyparrisus (see stories that follow this chapter), Apollo's boyhood friend. He was so filled with grief at killing the sun god's favorite stag that he died and was turned into a cypress tree.

In both North and South America most native peoples avoided cutting down living trees because they, like the Celts and Chinese, believed the trees had souls and could feel pain. Some tribes of the Pacific Northwest thought people who died a natural death dwelled as spirits in tall trees and so placed the bodies of their dead in the branches. The Iroquois, a northeastern tribe, tell the story of a boy who died from a fall; we will learn his story in chapter five. From his grave grew the first pine. It seems significant that myths and legends from many different cultures and areas of the world have such similar themes. Let's take a look at some theories that might explain this phenomenon.

Families of Races

It is thought that Celtic and Greek mythology are similar because the two cultures descend from the same Aryan race. The term Aryan refers to speakers of a group of languages which can be traced to a single source. They include all the various Greek, Roman, Slavic, German, Scandinavian and Celtic tribes as well as Indian, Persian, and other Asiatic groups. Similarities can be seen in the mythology and customs of all these societies because, in addition to language, the basis for their cosmologies is the same. The theme of the dying hero who changes into an evergreen was common in Asia Minor, where the Aryan race may have originated.

Diffusion

Chinese and Japanese are not generally considered to be of Aryan origin. Therefore, similarities between Aryan and Far Eastern culture are thought to come from contact between the groups in trade or travel. This assumption fits with the diffusion theory, popular among comparative folklorists. It states that a tale found in several forms in many different localities can be traced to one sophisticated culture where it was consciously created. Over the centuries the tale traveled from the parent society in arcing waves, similar to the pattern of concentric circles created when a pebble is dropped in a body of water. Because of contact between different peoples, the tale can cross cultural as well as geographic boundaries. Each society changes the story to fit its own purposes, but the basic symbols, patterns and motifs remain recognizable.

This theory might even explain similarities between folklore of the Old World and that found in the New. There is some evi-

dence that Asian travelers journeyed to both Alaska and South America, either by boat, or by foot when a land bridge existed between the continents where the Aleutian Islands are now. But what about similarities between folklore of peoples who most likely never met?

Psychology

Other theories about the origin of these stories come from the realm of psychology. Sigmund Freud noticed amazing similarities between the motifs found in the dreams of his patients and those found in myths and fairy tales. Even the dreams of small children who had little or no contact with the ancient stories contained similar patterns and symbols. He came to the conclusion that both dreams and myths contain products of a person's subconscious.

Psychologist Erich Fromm expanded on this theory. He postulated that humans reason, both consciously and subconsciously, by the use of analogy. Universal symbols arise from analogies made from basic human experiences such as birth, growth, sex, childbearing, and death, and outside happenings such as the change of seasons. According to Fromm, the symbols we choose to represent these worldwide experiences are the same because our process of reasoning is the same. However, occasionally universal symbols crop up in the dreams of children who have not as yet been exposed to the experiences from which some of these symbols are thought to originate.

Psychoanalyst Carl Jung theorized that the human mind contains a genetically inherited mental structure that creates those symbols which seem to be universal. This structure, which he called the "collective unconscious of the human race," contains memories of humankind's primordial past. Symbols which come from it, called "archetypes," sometimes seem to have no connection to an individual's personal past experiences.

Although widely believed, Jung's theories, until recently, seemed to have no known scientific foundation. Most biologists insist that memories and ideas can not be passed through the genes. They do admit, however, that there are certain phenomena that can not be explained by current scientific data and so-called "Laws of Nature." This can best be illustrated by the story of "the hundredth monkey."

Morphic Resonance

According to Ken Keyes, who popularized their findings, scientists have been conducting a study of the behavior of a species of Japanese monkey in the wild for over 30 years. During one part of the study they left raw sweet potatoes in the sand for the monkeys to eat. In 1952, on the island of Koshima, an 18 month-old female learned to wash her food in a nearby stream before eating it. Her mother and other young monkeys copied her.

By 1958 most of the young monkeys on this island washed their food. Adults who imitated their children also learned the trick but other adults did not. That autumn, an unknown number of these animals—99 is used for convenience—knew how to wash their potatoes. One day, one more—the hundredth monkey—learned, and by evening all but the oldest in the tribe were using the new behavior.

About that same time a seemingly impossible occurrence was recorded. Colonies of monkeys being studied on other islands and on the mainland at Takasakiyama spontaneously began to wash their food. It was as if the information had been sent over the water via telepathy. This could be thought of as just an extraordinary coincidence, except that similar observations have been recorded during experiments involving the synthesis of crystals, teaching rats to run mazes, and even teaching people from different nations to find hidden faces in pictures.

In 1981, botanist Rupert Sheldrake, in his book *A New Science of Life*, described a theory which would provide an explanation for these phenomena. The book created a major controversy because, if he is correct, the entire basis of current scientific thought would be challenged. Sheldrake proposes the existence of forces, which he calls "morphogenetic fields," which, like gravitational and electromagnetic fields, profoundly affect the growth and behavior of structures such as crystals, plants and animals. Like Jung's collective unconscious, these fields contain information from the near and distant past but, instead of residing within the structures they affect, they are entities themselves and remain separate. Through a process called "morphic resonance" similar structures, Japanese monkeys, for instance, might unconsciously alter morphogenetic fields. This information is then automatically communicated across time and space.

This idea is not new to the world of religion and philosophy. According to Hindu myth, the high god Indra once made a net with tiny bells attached at each intersection with which to enclose the earth. The slightest movement, even that which might be caused by a thought, was enough to set at least one bell ringing. Since the bells were so close together, one bell ringing would eventually cause all the others to ring, through a ripple effect. This story symbolized the belief that even thoughts could affect the universe because everything in the world is connected.

Religion and science are not often thought to be compatible but if Sheldrake's hypothesis is proven correct then not only can the existence of universal symbols and patterns in myths be scientifically explained, but also the spiritual power of prayer and ritual. Sheldrake has already received support from quantum physicists such as 1973 Nobel Prize winner Brian Josephson, who suspects that the expectations and thoughts of scientists might be influencing the outcome of their research. Recent experiments by Alain Aspect have shown that some kind of outside force or communication does seem to occur, at least, on the sub-atomic level.

Common Experiences

My own theory is that human beings share a great deal in common regardless of our cultures. When we're young we all depend on others for physical and emotional nurturance. We are all affected by the natural environment whether we live in the city or the country. We all develop patterns of behavior and ways of thinking that can be traced to a specific occurrence or series of occurrences. It does not matter if a young one has not been exposed to the actual experiences from which certain universal symbols are supposed to originate. The patterns of behavior and ways of looking at the world that come out of the experiences, and which provide the setting from which these symbols develop, can be passed on from society and parent to child. This phenomenon, plus the influence of contact between various cultures, could explain most similarities between mythical stories.

The evergreen as symbol of rebirth and eternal life is a key to the significance of the Christmas Tree. It is the one constant that links the earliest primeval associations to the story of Christ itself. As we explore pagan cosmologies in the next chapter, the importance of that connection becomes increasingly clear.

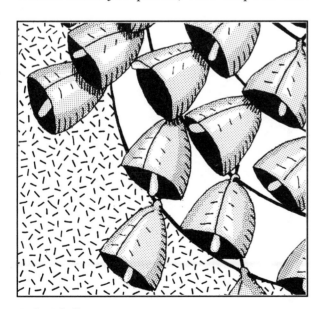

Indra's bells

The Pine of the Lovers

Japan

A faithful couple enjoyed many long years of happiness. They often told each other that they wished to remain together forever and hoped that one of them should never be left alone.

Their wish was granted. They died at the same time and their spirits were drawn into a tall pine tree of great age. This sacred pine had been planted by a god who had passed that way. On moonlit nights the old lovers may be seen raking together the pine needles under the tree. It is known as the Pine of the Lovers to this very day.

The Trees of Faithful Love

China

There once was a court official named Hanpang who had a very beautiful and loving wife. Many of the men who met her lusted after her, including the emperor himself. But she was very faithful.

The emperor was obsessed with her and decided he must have her for his own wife. He had her husband arrested on a false charge and sent to prison where he was tortured and given only small portions of moldy food to eat. The constant abuse and loneliness eventually overcame Hanpang. He became sick and soon died.

When his wife learned of this she was inconsolable. She wrote a letter asking to be buried in the same tomb as her husband and then committed suicide.

The emperor was furious. "If I cannot possess her neither shall he even unto death!" He did not respect her wishes and buried her a little distance away from her husband.

But the emperor's will was not as strong as that of heaven. In the night cedar trees grew up from the separate tombs. Within ten days the trees were so tall their branches interlaced as though they were embracing. The people called them the Trees of Faithful Love.

Cyparissus

Greece

When the god Apollo was just a boy he lived on the island of Ceos, off the coast of Greece near Athens. Ceos was a wonderful place with cool dense forests filled with magical beings. One of the nymphs who lived there tamed a beautiful stag. This magnificent animal was doted on by all the nymphs who decorated it with gold, silver, pearls and many precious stones.

The stag was well known to the people of Ceos and all the boys of the island loved it. But Apollo's closest friend Cyparissus loved it most of all. He spent as much time as he could with the animal and developed a special relationship with it. The stag gave him rides on its back when the boy was young. When he grew up Cyparissus helped protect it from harm and found it food.

The nymphs and satyrs found Cyparissus amusing and liked to tease him. They thought it great fun to attempt to steal his attention away from his unusual playmate. But whenever the nymphs would flirt with him or the satyrs tried to tempt him with wine and revelry, the youth just laughed and ran away.

When Cyparissus was not with the stag he practiced throwing the javelin with Apollo. He became such a skilled marksman that he could hit a running hare.

One day, while he was hunting, he saw a small and furry shape near the ground and began to stalk nearer to see what it was.

"It's a hare!" whispered the mischievous satyr Silenus in his ear. "Here's a test for you. Let's see if you are as clever with the javelin as they say. Can you hit so small a target at this distance? I doubt it!"

Cyparissus crept no closer. He took aim and hurled his weapon with all his might. His aim was true but, alas, it was no hare but his beloved stag laid down to rest in the shade.

When Cyparissus saw what he had done he was overcome with grief. He held the dying stag in his arms and wept and begged for death. The nymphs and satyrs could not comfort him. Not even the love of Apollo could help him recover.

"I will mourn for my friend until I die!" wept Cyparissus. "If only I could mourn him forever!"

Apollo granted his wish and turned him into a cypress tree. "I shall mourn you as you mourn for your stag." he said. "You will evermore mourn for others and be a companion of those in distress."

Ever since, the cypress tree has been planted in graveyards as a symbol of mourning and everlasting friendship.

The Old Man Who Made Trees Blossom

Japan

There once were two old couples who lived next door to each other. The first couple was kind and good but their neighbors were mean-spirited and hard. The kind old man and woman had a little white dog named Shiro who they loved very much. Their neighbors hated dogs and threw stones at the gentle animal.

One day Shiro was barking very loudly in the farmyard and was digging at the ground. The kind old man went to see what was the matter. "What is this you have found?" he asked. He got a spade and dug out a large pot. It was full of gold. The old man thanked his dog for leading him to this treasure and brought the money home.

His neighbor was watching all this and wanted to find gold, too. He asked if he could borrow Shiro. The good man would never refuse. "Of course, you may. I'm glad he may be of help to you."

The mean man took Shiro to his house and out to his field. "Find me some gold or I'll beat you." he said, yanking on the rope he had tied around Shiro's throat.

When Shiro started to dig at a certain spot, the old man tied the dog up and dug himself. All he found was foul smelling garbage. This made him so angry he hit Shiro on the head with the spade until he killed him.

The kind old man and woman were heartbroken and mourned for their little friend. They buried him in their field and planted a little pine tree over his grave so his spirit would be strong like the tree.

They visited Shiro's grave every day and tended to the tree carefully. The tree responded to their loving attention. In only a few years it had grown very big.

On the anniversary of Shiro's death the kind old man had a dream. He told his wife, "Remember how Shiro used to love to eat rice cakes? I dreamt that we should cut down the big pine tree and make a mortar to make rice cakes in Shiro's memory. I know we do not have much rice left but this is what I feel is right to do."

They cut down the tree that morning and made a mortar out of its trunk. Then they put a little steamed rice in it and began pounding it to make rice cakes. The rice multiplied. It seemed to be welling up from the bottom. From that day on, the aged couple never had to worry about lack of food, for the mortar provided for them whenever they used it.

The mean old man regularly spied on his neighbors so he saw the rice increase. One day he asked if he could borrow the utensil. The good couple let him and when he brought the mortar home he put a little steamed rice in it. "Watch this, wife. When I pound this rice it will make more rice." But when he demonstrated, the rice turned mouldy and full of worms instead. He was so angry he broke the mortar into small pieces and threw them into the fire.

When the kind old man went to retrieve the mortar he sorrowfully discovered that it was burned to ashes. The mortar reminded him of Shiro so he asked for the ashes and took them home with him.

He decided to scatter some of the ashes in his garden. It was winter and the trees were all bare, but when he scattered the ashes the cherry trees began to bloom. Everyone came to marvel at this wonderful sight—cherry blossoms in winter! Even the lord of the region came to see.

The lord had a cherry tree in his garden he loved very much. But when spring came the tree was dead. He sent for the kind old man and asked if he could bring his favorite tree back to life. The old man took some of the ashes from Shiro's mortar and threw them up into the dead branches. The tree was immediately covered with beautiful blossoms.

The lord was very happy and gave the old man presents and the honor of a new name, "Old-Man-Who-Makes-Trees-Blossom." The mean old man was jealous and told the lord he could do just as well. But when he threw the ashes into the trees they blew into the nobleman's eyes. Thinking he was insulted, he ordered the jealous man whipped.

The good old man and woman were now very rich and lived happily for many more years.

"The Tree of Life," Persian rug

CHAPTER FOUR

The Tree at the Center of the Universe

Then I was standing on the highest mountain of them all, and round about beneath me was the whole hoop of the WORLD. And while I stood there I saw more than I can tell and I understood more than I saw; for I was seeing in a sacred manner the shapes of all things in the spirit, and the shape of all shapes as they must live together like one being. And I saw that the sacred hoop of my people was one of many hoops that made one circle, wide as daylight and as starlight, and in the center grew one mighty flowering tree to shelter all the children of one mother and one father. And I saw that it was holy.
—Black Elk, BLACK ELK SPEAKS

Visualizations of the Universe

The cosmology of most primal peoples was based on the idea that, rather than a straight line ending in death, life was a cycle with no beginning nor end. Proof of this theory could be seen in nature every day of the year. The sun died daily and was reborn daily, while the moon went through the same cycle on a monthly basis. The most profound series of yearly occurrences, the change of the seasons, showed that all of nature could seem to die in the winter yet be born again in the spring.

Not only was death not the end of life, death was necessary for life to continue. When a predator killed another animal, the death of one perpetuated the life of the other. Any farmer knew that dead plants and other waste materials made perfect compost with which to rejuvenate the soil and produce more living plants. It was obvious to even the most superficial observer that the essence of life within every living thing did not disappear when the body died; it returned again or continued to exist in a different form.

This same view of life was reflected in early concepts of the universe. In various cultures the universe was symbolized as a circle or series of concentric circles, as a wheel, or a sphere. The *Rig Veda,* the most sacred literature of the Hindus, describes the universe as expanding infinitely outward in a circular fashion from a central point. This central axis was the most sacred element of all. It was the origin of the universe, sometimes thought to be a concentration of energies or the life principle, sometimes called God or the home of God or the gods.

Another example of the ancients' pervasive concept of the circularity of things is found in the way that most civilizations traced their own origins. They identified their beginnings in a central point, which they generally believed was located in the middle of the region in which they currently lived. Overlaps between these regions

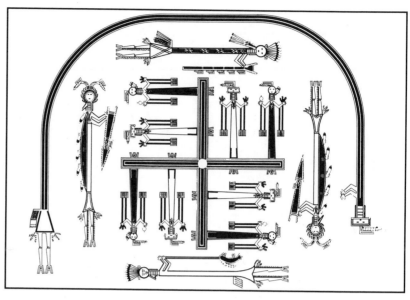

Navajo sand painting. Black cross-bars represent pine logs; the circle water. Figures of gods with their wives (goddesses) sit upon the logs. Round heads denote male; rectangular heads, female. Rattles and pinon sprigs bring male and female rains which bring forth vegetation. Arching over all is the rainbow goddess upon which the gods travel.

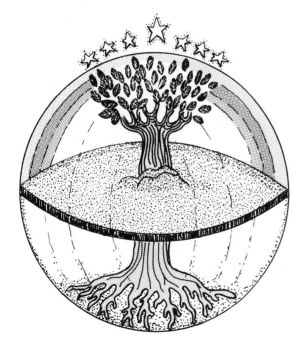

were not a point of contention among societies that lived in close contact with one another. All of the oriental civilizations, such as Mesopotamia, India and China, recognized an unlimited number of central axis points. This is not hard to understand if one thinks of the universe as a sphere of existence which, like all spheres, can have an infinite number of axes.

A common visualization of the universe consists of a sphere cut in half by a horizontal plane and intersected vertically by a central axis pole. The plane is the earth, the dome above is heaven, and the dome below is hell. The axis pole is the connecting point between all planes of existence. For those cultures which believe in these three cosmic regions, the central axis is the place where communication and passage between the three regions can happen. When the body of a person dies and the soul of that person is ready to go on to another form of existence, in heaven or hell or even on earth, it first must return to this central passageway.

The central axis was symbolized in a variety of ways, as a pole, pillar, column, ladder, mountain, pyramid and—significantly—as a cross, but the most popular symbol was that of the sacred tree. The three main portions of its structure joined the three cosmic regions: the roots went down to hell, the trunk grew on earth, and the branches reached toward heaven. The tree embodied the principles of life because it grew and regenerated itself. It lived a long time by human standards.

The tree was also associated with the four supreme elements: earth, water, air, and fire. It was born from the womb of the earth and was nourished by water. It reached up into the air and was, occasionally, struck by lightning creating fire, kindred to the sun. The many branches and leaves or needles represented the diversity of nature, while the one trunk from which they stemmed proved the unity of the whole. The evergreen promised that the life principles the tree represented were eternal. A grove of sacred trees, especially evergreens, was therefore a particularly spiritual place.

As indicated earlier, the return to the tree at death is common in myth and fairy tale. Birth from the tree is equally well known. In ancient Persia the story was told of the first two people growing up as a double tree with

"Nude Woman with the Zodiac," woodcut by Albrecht Dürer

the fingers of one curled over the ears of the other. When the tree reached maturity they were separated by the god Ormuzd. Similarly, the Romans and Greeks called oak trees the first mothers because, according to their mythology, the oak produced the first people.

Surviving to this day are several popular German fairy tales about the benevolent Mother Holda or Frau Holle, who lives in the forest. This figure comes from the ancient goddess Holda, part woman and part tree, who gave birth to humankind. She is described as appearing in human form from the

"The Gods of the Five World Directions," Aztec, Pre-Columbian. From Mayer Fejérváry Codex.

waist up in a doorway in the trunk of the great tree at the center of the earth. She receives the souls of men at death and allows them to emerge from the underworld at birth.

Gardens of Eden

Some students of anthropology and folklore suggest that primitive peoples really believed they descended from trees. It seems more likely that, if the tree was a symbol for the life-giving essences of the center, then stories telling how people were born of a tree simply symbolize the idea that the origin of humankind was from the same life essences that created and support the whole universe. An example of this comes from Aztec mythology.

The Aztec paradise, Tamoanchan, was situated in the highest of the thirteen heavens, atop a mountain almost tall enough to touch the moon. Being the home of the Earth Mother, Xochiquetzal or Precious Flower, it was an amazingly beautiful place. All the gods, as well as mortals, were created there and lived in perfect contentment, eating maize, the holy food. In the center of this land stood a tree whose boughs were not supposed to be broken or its flowers plucked. Exotic birds flitted and sang among its leaves without cease.

One day some of the lesser gods defied the taboo attached to the tree by tearing off long sprays of its flowers. The tree cracked and bled, losing forever its perfect health. As a result the gods were cast out of Tamoanchan to serve in the underworld, on earth and in the sky.

Tamoanchan is sometimes represented in Aztec art by a split tree. Because the home of the human race is represented by this tree, some tribes such as the Mixtecas called themselves "descendants of the tree." It is also interesting to note that within the Aztec paradise were two symbols of the center, the tree and the mountain. This is typical of most paradise stories the world over.

The Hindus called their sacred center *Idavarsha* or the Garden of Ida. Mount Meru,

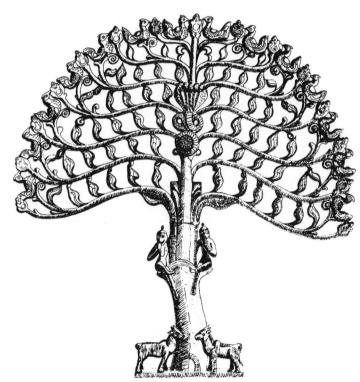

Tree of Life and Knowledge, bronze, India, Vigayanagas Period (1336-1546)

the mountain that held up the heavens and was home for the gods, was at the center. The slopes of the mountain collected the waters of heaven, the Ganges, and deposited them in Lake Manasasarovara, from which flowed the four rivers of the earth. This was also the home of the two trees of cosmic life—the *Kalpadruma* or Tree of the Ages and the *Parajita* or Tree of Every Perfect Gift.

Ancient Persian literature called the sacred garden *Aryana-Vaego.* Their Mount Meru, *Hara-Berezaiti,* provided a base for the bridge, *Kinvad,* which stretched over hell to heaven. The Tree of Healing and Immortality, the white *Homa* tree, grew within the garden near a fountain called *Arduisura,* from which the rivers Arvand and Daitya flowed to fill all the rivers and seas of the earth. On the top of the Homa tree sat *Simurg,* the Saena bird, who shook down from the tree the seeds of life for all living things. Another bird, *Kamros,* sat on top of Mount Hara-Berezaiti watching for the seeds to fall. When they did, he swooped down to carry them off and scatter them over the whole world.

Perhaps the most elaborate description of the sacred center comes from Scandinavia. In this cosmology the gods assembled atop the mountain called *Asgard,* which rose from the center of *Midgard,* the earth, to just below *Valhalla,* the Norse heaven. Valhalla could be reached only via *Bifrost,* the rainbow bridge. The massive trunk of the sacred evergreen ash *Yggdrasil* ran through and supported Midgard and then sprouted from the top of Asgard reaching ever upward to above the highest heavens, where it branched out and enveloped the entire universe.

The tree had three roots fixed deep in the underworld realm of *Hela.* Around them coiled the terrible serpent Nidhogg, who threatened to destroy the tree with his incessant gnawing. The first root went to *Niflheim,* the land of ice, to the Hvergelmir fountain, which fed all the rivers of the world. The second reached through the home of the giants to Mimir's Well, the fountain of wisdom. The third drank from Urd's Well, the fountain of youth, which was guarded by the *Norns,* or Fates, who governed the course of time and destiny. Yggdrasil was sometimes called "The Tree of Destiny." The budding and defoliating of the boughs represented every event in every land and every time. As a whole, the branches displayed the histories of all nations. The rustling of the leaves was the noise of human existence.

At the top of Yggdrasil sat a golden cock whose job it was to keep watch and warn the gods should their enemies, the giants, prepare to attack them. Beside it sat an eagle with a hawk perched between its eyes who kept watch over the whole world. A goat named Heidrun and four stags ate the leaves off the tree, while a squirrel named Ratatosk ran up and down, chattering, and creating discord between the eagle at the top and the serpent at the bottom.

This construction of a universe supported by a tree was reflected in early German architecture. Builders often used a central tree trunk or high beam driven into the ground to support the whole framework of a building.

Even though its existence seems delicately balanced, the ash Yggdrasil was a powerful Tree of Life, a symbol of strength and vitality.

During winter celebrations the tree was represented by an evergreen such as the fir. This made it easy for the Catholic church to connect the Scandinavian Yggdrasil with the Judeo-Christian interpretation of the biblical Tree of Life, also thought to be a fir or pine.

The Semitic Old Testament tells how the first man and woman were created within the Garden of Eden, a grove where every beautiful and food-bearing tree grew. At its center were the Tree of Life and the Tree of Knowledge. They were watered by a river which separated into four streams, the Pishon, the Gihon, the Tigris, and the Euphrates.

From this description it is theorized that the story of the Garden of Eden shares a common root with that of the Grove of Eridhu, mythological birthplace of the Babylonians, Sumerians and Akkadians. These peoples also claim their origins at the mouth of the Tigris and Euphrates rivers. Their mythology states that this is where the sky-god Anu modeled the first humans from clay. There Enki, the god of deep water, breathed life into their bodies. Enki's temple, the House of Wisdom, was located within the garden, as was the sacred *kiskana* tree, the Tree of Life, also known as the Black Pine of Eridhu.

Assyrian winged Genii gathering fruits (pine cones?) from the Tree of Life.

The Great Epic of Ancient Chaldea, written in about 2000 B.C., described the Grove of Eridhu as a forest of pines and cedars. A man named Izdubar journeyed to the grove to overthrow a tyrant, Khumbaba, who had conquered his land. Once in the grove Izdubar marvels at the sacred tree and its surroundings: "He saw the land of the Pine trees, the seat of the gods, the sanctuary of the angels. In front of the seed the Pine tree carried its fruit, good was its shadow, full of pleasure, an excellent tree, the choice of the forest."

Because the story of the Garden of Eden very likely came from a combination of Indian and Babylonian cosmologies, the early Hebrews probably thought the Tree of Life was a pine. It is known that before the time of the prophets, when the Israelites set up a sanctuary, they placed the altar under a green tree, as did their neighbors to the east and north. They also borrowed the Near Eastern Tree of Life symbol for the design of the traditional menorah. The idea that the tree might have been a pine was certainly familiar to them and to the Christians who came after.

Mystical Experiences

In Chapter Three we examined several theories that might explain the startling similarities between myths from different cultures. The stories that describe the great tree in the center of Paradise are so unusually complex and imaginative in description, however, that they warrant a closer look. Even with the information about what evergreen trees symbolized in the ancient world, it is hard to imagine what common experi-

ence could possibly give rise to the idea of a tree being the passageway people emerge from at birth and return to at death. Even though there are few other elements of the natural world that appear to reach to the underworld and up to heaven, it seems too big a leap of the imagination to use that as the sole origin of this almost universal concept.

Richard Heinberg, in his book *Memories and Visions of Paradise,* explores the theories of the origins of the paradise myths in depth. One of the more controversial theories relates to current research on near death experiences—the visions of people who survived after being at the brink of death.

The descriptions of near death experiences (NDEs) researchers have collected are remarkable not only in their similarity to each other but also to the descriptions of Paradise found in ancient myths. In general, the accounts include the same sequence of elements:

The dying person feels himself leave his body and travels through a long tunnel. At the end of the tunnel is an intensely beautiful place filled with a dazzling bright light. It is populated by radiant beings, some of whom the dying person recognizes as the spirits of family and friends who have already died. The beings radiate love, joy and complete knowledge, which the dying person sees as being part of his own nature as well. The experience of being in this place is one of total love, illumination and peace. Despite feelings of wanting to stay, the person returns to his physical body and lives.

In almost every case, the individuals who remember NDEs report profound changes in

Hieronymus Bosch, "Garden of Earthly Delights" (c. 1500). Left Panel.

their attitudes and values following their experience. They tend to have a greater sense of the sacredness of life and their connectedness with all living things. Their love and compassion for others is intensified while interest in personal status and material possessions declines. This change is apparent to family and friends as well as to themselves.

With medical advances making revivals of nearly dead individuals more frequent, reports of NDEs are becoming more common. Researchers are divided over whether NDEs are descriptions of an afterlife or are the result of biochemical processes in the brain. Regardless of origin they do seem to fit into a family of mystical experiences that prophets, yogis, mystics and saints have reported throughout history. These experiences result from dreams, deep meditation, hypnotic states and other forms of altered consciousness.

There is plenty of room for speculation when it comes to information of this kind. It does, however, suggest an interesting explanation for the universal Tree of Life symbol. Several of the stories describe the trunk of the tree as hollow. A hollow tree would be a good analogy for the tunnel reported in NDEs.

The true strength of myths, legends and fairy tales lies in the preservation and communication of the values and attitudes of the societies in which they are told. The basic outlook shared by survivors of near death experiences and spiritual leaders of many backgrounds—the sacredness and unity of an ever-living world—is at the heart of all the ancient traditions. Through hearing or reading the tales of our ancestors we may regain the knowledge they had to share: that we as humans are inherently connected to each other, to the earth, and to all the creatures of the earth.

Regardless of origin, the Tree of Life is a powerful symbol. The Christmas Tree is clearly connected to it, but the significance goes further. The pine tree plays an important role in the closest ancestor to the Christ story, the myth of the Earth Mother and her son, the Dying God, which we will explore in depth in the next chapter.

The First Dogs

Aztec, Mexico and Central America

The god Tezcatlipoca learned that the world was to be destroyed in a great flood. He appeared to a man named Tata and a woman named Nene and warned them of the danger to come.

"Climb to the top of the giant fir tree," he commanded them. "Each of you take an ear of holy maize. If you eat but one kernel a day you may survive."

When the waters finally receded, the two mortals climbed down from the tree to prepare for their new life. All the goddesses and gods peered down from heaven to see what they would do.

One of the first things they did was gather fish to eat. As they did so one of the gods dropped some heavenly fire by mistake. Disregarding the sacred nature of their find, the people used the fire to burn the wood of the tree to cook their fish.

Looking down from the heavens the two high gods, Citlallatonac and Citlalicue, were outraged. "What is the meaning of this smoke? Don't they realize that fire belongs to the gods alone? How dare they burn the tree!"

They sent Tezcatlipoca down to punish the humans for their sacrilege. Tezcatlipoca did this by decapitating them and sticking their heads on their rear ends. They thus ceased to be human and changed into dogs.

The Juniper Tree

Collected by the Brothers Grimm, Germany

Long, long ago, maybe as much as two thousand years ago, there lived a rich man and his beautiful and pious wife. They loved each other very much and were very happy, but they had no children. They wished greatly for some children, and the pious wife prayed day and night.

In the courtyard in front of their house stood a juniper tree. One winter day the wife was standing beneath it paring an apple when she cut her finger. Drops of her blood fell upon the snow.

"Ah," sighed the woman, looking down at the blood, "if only I could have a child as red as blood, and as white as snow!"

As she said these words her heart grew light, and she felt certain that her wish had been granted. So she went back into the house, and when a month had passed the snow was gone; in two months everything was green; in three months flowers sprang up out of the earth; in four months the trees were in full leaf, and the branches were thickly entwined; the little birds began to sing, so that the woods echoed, and the blossoms fell from the trees; when the fifth month had passed the wife stood under the juniper tree, and it smelt so sweet that her heart leaped within her, and she fell on her knees for joy; and when the sixth month had gone, the fruit was thick and fine, and she remained still; and the seventh month she gathered the berries and ate them eagerly, and was sick and sorrowful; and when the eighth month had passed she called to her husband, and said, weeping, "If I die, bury me under the juniper tree."

Then she was comforted and happy until the ninth month had passed, and she bore a son as white as snow and as red as blood. When she saw him her joy was so great that she died.

Her husband buried her under the juniper tree and wept inconsolably. As time passed he became less sad and, after grieving a little while longer, he took another wife.

His second wife bore him a daughter who she loved dearly, but she could not look at her stepson without evil in her heart. She wanted to get all her husband's money for her daughter, but the little boy stood in the way. She grew to despise him and drove him from one corner to another, giving him a buffet here and a cuff there, so that the poor child was always in disgrace. When he came home from school there was no peace for him.

Once, when the wife went into the room upstairs, her little daughter followed her, saying, "Mother, give me an apple."

"Yes, my child," said her mother. She gave her a fine apple out of the chest with the great heavy lid and the strong iron lock.

"Mother," said the little girl, "shall not my brother have one too?"

"Yes," she replied, "when he comes back from school." Just then she looked out the window and saw the boy coming, and an evil thought crossed her mind. She snatched the apple away from her daughter, saying, "You shall not have it before your brother."

Then she threw the apple into the chest and slammed down the lid. The little boy came in at the door, and she said to him in a kind tone, but with evil looks, "My son, would you like an apple?"

"Mother," said the boy, "you look terrible! Yes, I would like an apple."

Then she spoke as kindly as before, holding up the cover of the chest, "Come here and take out one for yourself."

As the boy stooped over the open chest, crash went the lid down, so that his head flew off among the red apples. But then the woman felt great terror and wondered how she could escape the blame. She fit the head to the neck, and bound them with a handkerchief, so that nothing could be seen. She set him on a chair before the door with the apple in his hand.

Then little Marjory came into the kitchen to her mother, who was standing before the fire stirring a pot of hot water.

"Mother," said Marjory, "my brother is sitting by the door and he has an apple in his hand, and he looks very pale. I asked him to give me the apple, but he did not answer me. It's so strange!" "Go to him again," said the mother, "and if he still does not answer you, give him a box on the ear."

So Marjory went again and said, "Brother, give me the apple."

But as he took no notice, she gave him a box on the ear, and his head fell off, at which she was horrified, and began to cry and scream. She ran to her mother and said, "Oh mother! I have knocked my brother's head off!" and she cried and screamed without cease.

"Oh Marjory!" said her mother, "What have you done? But keep quiet so that no one may see there is anything the matter. It can't be helped now; we will put him out of the way safely."

When the father came home and sat down at the table, he said, "Where is my son?" But the mother was filling a great dish full of black broth, and Marjory was crying bitterly, for she could not refrain. Then the father said again, "Where is my son?" "Oh," said the mother, "he is gone into the country to his great-uncle's to stay for a little while." "What for?" said the father, "and without bidding me good-bye?" "Oh, he wanted to go so much, and he asked me to let him stay there six weeks; he will be well taken care of." "Dear me," said the father, "I am quite sad about it; it was not right of him to go without bidding me good-bye."

With that he began to eat, saying, "Marjory, what are you crying for? Your brother will be back."

After a while he said, "Well, wife, the food is very good; give me some more."

And the more he ate the more he wanted, until he had eaten it all, and he threw the bones under the table. Then Marjory got one of her best handkerchiefs, and picked up all the bones from under the table and tied them up in it. She went outside with them, crying bitterly, and laid them in the green grass under the juniper tree. Immediately her heart grew light again, and she wept no more.

Then the juniper tree began to wave to and fro, and the boughs drew together and then parted, just like hands clapping for joy; then a cloud rose from the tree, and in the midst of the cloud there burned a fire, and out of the fire a beautiful bird arose. It sang most sweetly, soared high into the air, and flew away. When it was gone the juniper tree stood as before, but the handkerchief full of bones was gone. Marjory felt quite glad and light-hearted, just as if her brother was still alive. So she went back merrily into the house and had her dinner.

The bird, when it flew away, perched on the roof of a goldsmith's house, and began to sing,

"It was my mother who murdered me;
It was my father who ate me;
It was my little sister Marjory
Who gathered up my bones,
Wrapped them in a handkerchief,
And laid them under the juniper tree.
Kyweet, kyweet, kyweet, I cry,
Oh, what a beautiful bird am I!"

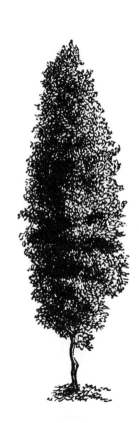

The goldsmith was sitting in his shop making a golden chain, but when he heard the bird, he stopped his work and went out to the street to listen so quickly he lost a slipper along the way and stood there in the sun with only one slipper on, the gold chain in one hand and his pincers in the other.

"Bird," he said, "how beautifully you sing. Do sing that piece again." "No," said the bird, "I do not sing for nothing twice; if you will give me that gold chain I will sing again." "Very well," said the goldsmith, "here is the chain; now do as you said."

Down came the bird and took the gold chain in his right claw, perched in front of the goldsmith, and sang,

"It was my mother who murdered me;
It was my father who ate me;
It was my little sister Marjory
Who gathered up my bones,
Wrapped them in a handkerchief,
And laid them under the juniper tree.
Kyweet, kyweet, kyweet, I cry,
Oh, what a beautiful bird am I!"

Then the bird flew to a shoemaker's, and perched on his roof, and sang,

"It was my mother who murdered me;
It was my father who ate me;
It was my little sister Marjory
Who gathered up my bones,
Wrapped them in a handkerchief,
And laid them under the juniper tree.
Kyweet, kyweet, kyweet, I cry,
Oh, what a beautiful bird am I!"

When the shoemaker heard, he ran outside in his shirt sleeves and looked up at the bird who sat on the roof of his house. "Bird," he said, "how beautifully you sing!" Then he called his wife and children and all his acquaintances to come and listen to the bird. So they did and stood and stared to see how beautiful it was with red and green feathers, a golden throat and eyes that twinkled like stars.

"Bird," said the shoemaker, "do sing that piece again." "No," said the bird, "I may not sing for nothing twice; you must give me something." So the shoemaker asked his wife to bring the pair of red shoes he had just made to give to the bird. "Now bird," said the man, "sing us that piece again."

And the bird came down and took the shoes in his left claw, and flew up again to the roof, and sang,

"It was my mother who murdered me;
It was my father who ate me;
It was my little sister Marjory
Who gathered up my bones,
Wrapped them in a handkerchief,
And laid them under the juniper tree.
Kyweet, kyweet, kyweet, I cry,
Oh, what a beautiful bird am I!"

And when he had finished he flew away, with the chain in his right claw and the shoes in his left. He flew until he reached a mill where sat twenty miller's men hewing a millstone. The bird sat on the branch of a linden tree which stood in front of the mill, and sang,

"It was my mother who murdered me..."

Here one of the men looked up.

"It was my father who ate me..."

Then two more looked up and listened.

"It was my little sister Marjory..."

Here four more looked up.

"...Who gathered up my bones,
Wrapped them in a handkerchief..."

Now there were only eight left hewing.

"...And laid them under the juniper tree."

Now only five.

"Kyweet, kyweet, kyweet, I cry,"

Now only one.

"Oh, what a beautiful bird am I!"

At length the last one left off, and he heard only the end.

"Bird," said he, "how beautifully you sing; let me hear it all. Sing that again!" "No," said the bird, "I may not sing it twice for nothing. If you give me the millstone I will sing it again." "Indeed," said the man, "if it belonged to me alone you should have it." "All right," said the others, "if he sings again he shall have it."

Then the bird came down, and all twenty millers heaved up the stone with poles—"Yo! Heave-ho! Yo! Heave-ho!" and the bird stuck his head through the hole in the middle, and with the millstone around his neck he flew up to the tree and sang,

"It was my mother who murdered me;
It was my father who ate me;
It was my little sister Marjory
Who gathered up my bones,
Wrapped them in a handkerchief,
And laid them under the juniper tree.
Kyweet, kyweet, kyweet, I cry,
Oh, what a beautiful bird am I!"

And when he had finished, he spread his wings, having in the right claw the chain, in the left the shoes, and around his neck the millstone, and he flew away to his father's house.

In the parlor sat the father, the mother, and Marjory at the table. The father said, "How light-hearted and cheerful I feel." "Nay," said his wife, "I feel very low, just as if a great storm were coming."

But Marjory sat weeping; and the bird came flying, and perched on the roof.

"Oh," said the father, "I feel so joyful, and the sun is shining so bright; it is as if I were going to meet with an old friend." "Nay," said the wife, "I am terrified, my teeth chatter, and there is fire in my veins," and she tore her dress open to get air. Marjory sat in a corner and wept, with her plate before her, until it was quite full of tears. Then the bird perched on the juniper tree and sang,

"It was my mother who murdered me..."

And the mother stopped her ears and hid her eyes so she would not see nor hear; but, the noise of a fearful storm was in her ears, and in her eyes a quivering and burning as of lightening.

"It was my father who ate me..."

"Oh, mother!" said the father, "there is a beautiful bird singing so finely, and the sun shines, and everything smells as sweet as cinnamon."

"It was my little sister Marjory..."

Marjory hid her face in her lap and wept, and the father said, "I must go out to see the bird." "Oh, do not go!" said the wife, "I feel as if the house were on fire."

But the man went out and looked at the bird.

"...Who gathered up my bones,
Wrapped them in a handkerchief,
And laid them under the juniper tree.
Kyweet, kyweet, kyweet, I cry,
Oh, what a beautiful bird am I!"

With that the bird dropped the gold chain so that it landed around his father's neck, fitting him perfectly. He went indoors and said, "Look what a beautiful chain the bird has given me!"

Then his wife was so terrified that she fell down on the floor, and her cap came off. Then the bird again began to sing,

"It was my mother who murdered me..."

"Oh," groaned the mother, "that I were a thousand fathoms under ground so that I would not have to hear it."

"It was my father who ate me..."

Then the woman lay as if she were dead.

"It was my little sister Marjory..."

"Oh," said Marjory, "I will go out, too, and see if the bird gives me anything." And so she went.

"...Who gathered up my bones,
Wrapped them in a handkerchief."

Then he threw the shoes down to her.

And laid them under the juniper tree.

"Kyweet, kyweet, kyweet, I cry,
Oh, what a beautiful bird am I!"

And poor Marjory all at once felt happy and joyful, and put on her red shoes, and danced and jumped for joy. "Oh dear," she said, "I felt so sad before I went outside, and now my heart is so light! He is a charming bird to have given me a pair of red shoes."

But the mother's hair stood on end and she said, "Even if the world is coming to an end, I must go outside for a little relief."

Just as she came outside the door, crash went the millstone on her head, and crushed her flat. The father and daughter rushed out, and saw smoke and flames of fire rise up; but when that had gone by, there stood the little brother. He took his father and Marjory by the hand, and they felt very happy and content, and went indoors, and sat at the table, and had their dinner.

The Tale of Bonchevalier

France

One Christmas Eve the knight Bonchevalier was riding through a deep forest. He came to a point in the path where he could see a far distance, and when he looked ahead he saw a very tall evergreen. It seemed to glow with lights and a star appeared to rest among its topmost branches.

Bonchevalier was amazed. As he came nearer he realized the tree was covered with candles. Some were upside down and others were upright. The star at the top of the tree was actually the glow of a beautiful child with a halo about his head. He did not know what to make of this.

When he got home he told his story but the wise men of the community were puzzled. However, his mother knew just what he had seen.

"What you saw was the Tree of Humanity." she said. "Good people are represented by the upright candles; the bad are the upside down ones. The child at the top is the infant Jesus who watches over people all over the world. France is truly blessed by your vision."

"The Virgin in Glory," woodcut by Albrecht Dürer .

CHAPTER FIVE

The Earth Mother and the Dying God

Venus, when her son was lost,
Cried him up and down the coast,
In hamlets, palaces, and parks,
And told the truant by his marks—
Golden curls, and quiver, and bow.
—Ralph Waldo Emerson, THE INITIAL LOVE

The cosmology of the universe was inherent in the myths most ancient peoples told of the gods and goddesses. One of the most common plots is that of the Earth Mother and her son, the Dying God. The events in the story vary from place to place but the basic elements clearly remain.

According to Otto Rank, a disciple of Freud, the archetypal myth of the hero contains the following elements: The infant hero is born of divine parents, or of the union of a deity and an earthly mother. The birth itself is difficult or extraordinary in some way. The baby is then exiled with his mother or is sent away to be raised by someone else. In his youth he goes through a harrowing adventure which results in his death in either a symbolic or figurative sense, and he is mourned by his mother until he returns. When he does, the hero either overthrows his father or is reconciled with him and completes his father's work.

Much has been written about the psychological symbolism in these myths, but for our purposes the *sequence* of events is the important thing, for it explains the turning of the seasons. Let's trace the evolution of versions of the myth most closely tied to the importance of the evergreen tree.

Aphrodite/Ishtar and Adonis/Tammuz

The worship of Aphrodite and Adonis, dating from the sixth or seventh century B.C., was especially popular in Greece. The same story crops up in Syria, Babylonia and Palestine, where the chief protagonists were known as Ishtar and Tammuz. According to this myth, Adonis was conceived of incest between the Syrian King Theias and his daughter Myrrha. Myrrha was turned into a myrrh tree soon afterwards, and ten months later her bark peeled off and the baby Adonis was born.

The goddess of love, Aphrodite, who was an Earth Mother in the sense that she represented the reproductive powers of the earth, adopted the little boy and, worried about his safety, hid him in a chest which she entrusted to Persephone, queen of the underworld.

When Persephone opened the chest and saw how beautiful the child was, she refused to give him back. Aphrodite, in despair, disconsolately made the long journey to the land of the dead to find and fight for her son. While she was gone, the power of love, fertility, faded from the world. Living things forgot to reproduce and plant life started to die.

To save the earth, Zeus put an end to the argument between the two women by deciding that Adonis would spend one-third of each year with Aphrodite, one third with Persephone, and another third wherever he pleased, which turned out to be with Aphrodite.

Another myth tells that one day Aphrodite was wounded by one of Cupid's arrows while they were playing. Before she was healed, Adonis came to see her and she instantly fell in love with him. She spent every moment she could with him, even joining him in hunting, not normally one of her favorite activities. She often begged him to be more careful and not hunt the more dangerous animals, but Adonis paid no attention.

One day, when the goddess was off attending to business she had neglected, the god Ares, who was in love with her and jealous of the time she spent with Adonis, sent a wild boar to attack him. Adonis managed to wound it with his spear, but the enraged animal pulled it out and drove its tusks into his side. Aphrodite heard Adonis cry out and rushed to his aid, but by the time she reached him he was already dead. She mourned loud and long, and, as a memorial, turned his blood into the anemone flower.

In the Syrian version of the tale, Tammuz (Adonis) dies and passes away to the underworld. After Ishtar goes to find him, the queen of the underworld, Allatu or Ereshkigal, allows her to use the waters of life to revive him and return to the upperworld to revive nature.

The rituals of the cults of Adonis and Tammuz suggest that all versions of the story were familiar to the participants. It is likely that the death of Adonis/Tammuz by the boar was interpreted as happening just at the time the god was supposed to join Persephone in the underworld, the time of year when living things appeared to die. His resurrection by

"Venus and Adonis," by Peter Paul Rubens, 1577-1640.

the waters of life coincided with the spring rains which yearly marked the rebirth of nature.

Each year in the springtime the River Adonis, located in Syria between Tripoli and Beirut, is stained blood-red by the red earth washed down from the mountains by the rain. In ancient times it was said to be the blood of Adonis, just killed by a boar on Mount Lebanon.

This event marked the start of the celebration of Adonis. An image of the god was carved of wood and placed inside a hollow tree. To mourn his death the image was wrapped in a shroud by women who accompanied the activity with wailing and bitter laments. In a long procession they carried the corpse-like statue or effigy down to the river or sea and threw it into the water. The revival of Adonis was usually celebrated the very next day.

Another custom, also chiefly maintained by women, involved planting baskets or pots of barley, wheat, lettuce, fennel and various flowers which were called the Gardens of Adonis. They were tended for eight days, during which time they grew very quickly. But after that time they died for lack of root space. The dead plants joined the images of Adonis as they were thrown into the water.

Social scientists point to these rituals as proof of the idea that the myths were symbolic interpretations of the change of seasons. Adonis, represented by the potted plants, was an anthropomorphic form of the vegetation loved and cared for by the earth, the Earth Mother. In a Babylonian hymn it was said that Tammuz dwelt in the midst of the great tree at the center of the earth. Like a tree, Adonis/Tammuz embodied the life essence which sustained the universe, and, like all who make the journey from earth to hell, the god was born from and returned to the great passageway, the central axis pole, the tree.

Cybele and Attis

During the same period of time and probably for several centuries before, the cult of Cybele and Attis flourished to the north in Asia Minor, especially in the great religious centers of Phrygia, Galatia and Lydia. It spread to Thrace and Greece, and,

Cybele/Agdistis.

in 204 B.C., was adopted by the Romans in response to an oracle which proclaimed that Italy could defeat Hannibal of Carthage if the Idaean Earth Mother, Cybele, were to be brought to Rome. The cult was one of the most popular at the time Christianity was introduced, and provided the new religion with some of its stiffest competition.

In this myth the great god Zeus lusted after the Earth Mother, Cybele, who hid from him in the form of a rock. While he was asleep, the frustrated god ejaculated upon the earth, which caused the hermaphrodite Agdistis to be born. Agdistis was a terrible and destructive monster.

To subdue the horrible creature, the god Dionysus drugged it with wine and tied its male genitals to a tree so that on awakening they would be pulled off. An almond tree grew from the spot where they fell. One day a nymph, Nana, picked an almond from this tree and placed it in her bosom. Several months later she gave birth to a son who she named Attis.

The boy grew up to be a very handsome young man, deeply loved by Cybele and lusted after by Agdistis, who became his lover. According to some versions of the story Cybele is Agdistis. In any case, Attis decided to marry Ia, the daughter of King Midas, in secret, but the Earth Mother discovered them. At the marriage ceremony the enraged Agdistis struck everyone with madness. Attis emasculated himself in the ensuing chaos and died.

While violets sprang up from his blood, his beloved Ia wrapped his body in wool and, in her grief, committed suicide. Attis was then carried to a cave by Cybele and Agdistis who mourned long and loud, begging Zeus to preserve him. Most renditions of the tale end with the dead man being changed into a pine tree.

During the rites of Attis, which took place over a period of four days in March, a pine tree was cut in the woods and brought to the sanctuary of Cybele, where it was wrapped like a corpse in woolen bands and decorated with garlands of violets. An effigy of Attis was tied to its trunk. Eunuch priests called *Galloi* chanting hymns and playing flutes, cymbals, tambourines and horns, then led a wild procession through the streets.

The ceremony was marked by frenzied dancing and bloodletting, which lasted until all were exhausted. The priests then buried the effigy and fasted from bread. The next day, which was the vernal equinox, the tomb was opened and it was proclaimed that the god had risen from the dead. This ritual ushered in the roman festival of *Hilaria,* a joyous carnival similar to the Mardi Gras.

One theory suggests that the birth, growth, self-castration and death of Attis represents the springing, growth and death of plant life. Attis represents, according to this interpretation, the plant kingdom beloved by Cybele; his emasculation is the harvesting of fruits; his death, burial and preservation symbolize the death and preservation of plant life in winter; his resurrection brings on the return of spring.

Dionysus and Jesus

The pattern of the hero is most clearly seen in the myth of Dionysus or Bacchus. Dionysus was the son of Zeus and a mortal woman Semele. Zeus' wife, Hera, was jealous of Semele. Appearing to her disguised as her handmaiden, Hera suggested to Semele that she ask her lover to reveal himself to her in all his splendor. Semele tricked Zeus into doing so, whereupon she was killed instantly by a thunderbolt. Fortunately, some cooling ivy tendrils protected the baby within her womb. Zeus took the fetus and stitched it into his thigh until it was ready to be born. Having matured within the body of a god, Dionysus was born a god himself and became Zeus' favorite child.

Bacchus on a wine vat.

Dionysus was brought up by the nymphs of Mount Nysa disguised as a young goat to protect him from Hera. When she eventually found him, Zeus sent the boy to the wine country where he discovered the cultivation of the vine. But Hera was relentless. She hounded him and drove him from place to place. This persecution drove him mad and he wandered about the countryside in a daze.

In time he came to Phrygia. There he met the goddess of wild nature, Cybele, who cured him and taught him her religious rites. He then set out to Asia to teach people the cultivation of the vine. Dozens of stories are told about Dionysus' adventures in India, Thrace and Greece.

Wherever he went he was accompanied by hordes of women known as the *bacchantes,* and also by *sileni,* who were half man and half horse, by the *satyrs,* who were half man and half goat, and other fertility deities who participated in his orgiastic rites. The adventure which explained his yearly death and resurrection was the account of his trip to Hades to find his mother, Semele, and bring her back to Olympus.

Another version of the story of Dionysus claims that he was born on December 25. He became the god of wine as a child, and as such performed miracles like turning water into wine. Hera lured him into a trap where her cohorts, the Titans, rushed upon him, tore him limb from limb, boiled his body with various herbs and ate it.

But Dionysus' sister Athena kept his heart and gave it to Zeus, telling him the whole story. In his rage, the god put the Titans to

Roman Sarcophagus showing Dionysus, Pan, satyrs, etc.

death by torture. He made an image in which he enclosed his child's heart and then built a temple in his honor. In another version, Zeus swallows the heart and then uses Semele to father him again. However it happened, Dionysus was supposed to have either risen up to heaven or been revived on March 25.

Just as Dionysus suffered in the myth, the vine which represents him seems to suffer as well. Each autumn, grape vines are pruned back so far that all that remains is a dead-looking stalk. It seems incredible that the plant could come back to life in the spring, but it does. This event was celebrated as the resurrection of Dionysus at the Greek new year in March. During the processional a baby, representing the newly reborn god, was carried in a place of honor.

Then the wild Bacchanalian rites began, with the drinking of large quantities of wine, frenzied dancing, singing and sexual abandon. Sometimes a wild animal was torn apart and eaten raw. The aim of the worshippers was to become one with Dionysus by losing their conscious selves to their wilder natures and by symbolically taking the god within their bodies. The proper state was accomplished by drinking enough wine.

The god of the vine has an interesting connection with the pine tree. The grape seemed to flourish best in places where the pine liked to grow. Pine resin was used to conserve wine and refine it, and sometimes wine was brewed from its seeds.

When the Delphic oracle commanded the Corinthians to worship the pine tree equally with the god Dionysus, the evergreen became an important symbol. Images of the god were made of pine wood, draped in a mantle, with a bearded mask to represent the head and with leafy boughs projecting from the body. During nighttime celebrations, pine torches illuminated the scene, and each worshipper carried a wand, called the *thyrsus*, which was tipped with a pine cone. The pine cone was a common symbol of fertility, used in the cult of Venus or Aphrodite, and was thought to have power over the fruits of the earth and the womb. Contemporary bedposts from the last century were often adorned with carved pine cones for this reason.

It is important to realize that, more than anything else, Dionysus was a god of fertility. His cult differed from previous ones in that it stressed the male god's power to influence nature more than the strength of the Earth Mother. His popularity indicates the Greeks' attitude toward women at that time. Transferring the power of fertility to the male was significant in the evolution of religion. It paved the way for the Christ story which, although it contains several elements of the earlier stories, almost entirely eliminates the role of the Earth Mother. Mary, a mortal woman, attains her special holiness only by virtue of being chosen to be the carrier and caretaker of the infant male god.

Connections can clearly be seen between the stories of Christ and Dionysus. Jesus was the long-awaited hero, the Messiah born on the winter solstice through the intervention of God and the Holy Virgin. After teaching humankind important spiritual lessons, he was killed by dark forces only to be resurrected in the spring. In an early painting Jesus is shown suffering on a cross overgrown with grapevines and clusters of grapes. This reference to Dionysus is repeated in the Gospel of John 15: 1-2 where Jesus declares, "I am the true vine, and my Father is the vinedresser."

With the rapid spread of Christianity, pagan beliefs about the universe and their relationship with the sacred tree underwent a great transformation. When one becomes aware of that transformation and how it was achieved, it is little wonder that the original significance of the tree was all but lost.

"Christ as a Cluster of Grapes" based on detail of a church door, Castle of Valére, Sion, Switzerland.

Ivan Sosnovich
Soviet Union

Once upon a time there was an old couple whose only regret in life was that they had no children. After years of prayers and tears, the old woman said to her husband that there was only one thing left to do. He must go into the forest, cut down a fine piece of pine wood, and carve it into the likeness of a boy. This he did and brought back to his wife. For three years the old woman rocked the wooden image in a cradle and cooed to it as if it were alive

One day as the woman was preparing a meal to take to her husband in the fields a miraculous transformation occurred. Warmth spread through the body of the wooden child, and its hard stiff limbs became soft and flexible. The boy opened his eyes and hopped to his feet.

"Mother!" he cried, "I'm alive." He walked over to the astonished and delighted woman and took her hands. "My name is Ivan Sosnovich (John Pineson)."

Ivan grew up to be a mighty and daring man who had many amazing adventures.

The Dancing Brothers
Iroquois tribe, North America

Long ago there lived seven brothers who, on hot summer nights, slept outside their hogan in the cool grass. One night they were awakened by the most beautiful singing. It seemed to be coming from the stars.

The sound enveloped the brothers, lifting them up and lightening their very souls. They began to dance a rhythmic weaving dance in the soft moonlit night. Entering a trancelike state they danced and danced until they found themselves climbing up into the sky.

The youngest brother was the first to pull his attention away. "My brothers! Look at where we are!" he exclaimed. "How can this be? Why are we here?"

"You have been chosen to be stars in the heavens," answered the moon. "In the season of the new year, when the council fires are lit, you shall dance over the lodges of your people."

The moon raised his arm to set the brothers into the sky, but the youngest suddenly became distraught because he could hear the sound of a woman weeping.

"That's our mother!" he cried. He turned to look back and fell out of the sky. His body struck the earth with such force it was buried deep in the ground.

His mother watered his grave with her tears every day for many long months. One day a tiny green sprout sprang up from the earth at that very spot. Before the amazed woman's eyes it grew larger and larger, becoming a towering pine tree, full with branches and pointing to the other brothers in the sky.

The Day the Sun Disappeared
Japan

The sun goddess, Amaterasu, was the most beautiful of all the goddesses and the most generous with her love for the earth and all its creatures. She shone in the sky and presided over heaven.

Her younger brother was the storm god Susanowo. He was dark and gloomy, very strong and bad-tempered. His domain was the sea.

Susanowo fought with his sister constantly. He longed to live with his mother and resented his sister's place of honor. Amaterasu did her best to keep the world orderly and full of life and light, but her brother would roar through the land destroying all he could see.

One day the storm god decided to visit his sister in heaven. When Amaterasu saw him coming, she thought he planned to usurp her domain and met him fully armed and prepared to do battle. Susanowo convinced her that he had no evil intentions. He had come to make peace with her before traveling to see their mother. They agreed to exchange their possessions and beget children.

The sun goddess gave her jewels to her brother and he gave her his sword. They both drank from the heavenly well and put the things they had exchanged into their mouths. Out of the sword in Amaterasu's mouth came the goddess of rapids and whirlpools and a beautiful boy who became her favorite son. Out of the jewels in Susanowo's mouth came the gods of light and vitality.

For a time the earth was peaceful. Growing things flourished, evil spirits were confined, men gathered full crops and celebrated the harvest rites. But then Susanowo became restless again.

The god ran riot on the earth stripping branches and leveling trees. He destroyed the rice fields built by his sister and polluted her holiest observances. Finally Amaterasu could bear it no longer and hid in a cave on Mount Kagu. The source of light thus disappeared. The world became dark and plagued by the evil spirits who could no longer be contained.

The eight millions of gods assembled in front of the cave and consulted among themselves how light might be restored. They tried every divine remedy they could think of and brought forth mirrors, swords and cloth offerings with which to gather and direct their combined power. A pine tree called the "sakaki" was set up and decorated with jewels, mirrors and strings. Cocks kept up a perpetual crowing and bonfires were lit. Then the goddess Uzume performed a dance so amusing that the laughter of the assembled gods filled the air and made the earth tremble.

The sun goddess heard the merry noise and was curious. But no sooner had she opened a small hole to peep out than a powerful god widened it and pulled her out while the other gods blocked her from slipping back into the cave.

Thus the sun reappeared. The universe was once more brightly illuminated and evil vanished. Order and peace prevailed on the earth once more.

CHAPTER SIX

The Death of Pan

...And that dismal cry rose slowly
And sank slowly through the air,
Full of spirit's melancholy
And eternity's despair!
And they heard the words it said -
Pan is dead! Great Pan is dead!
Pan, Pan is dead!
—Elizabeth Barrett Browning, *The Dead Pan*

Arcadia, a beautiful land of pine-covered mountains, was the favorite dwelling place of the beloved god of nature, Pan. A fun-loving god, Pan spent his days frolicking and pursuing game in the valleys with the satyrs and dancing under the trees with the nymphs. He invented the shepherd's pipe, and many a traveler through the sacred groves claimed to have heard him play.

Pan means "all," an appropriate name for one who represented the entire universe. His hairy legs with feet hoofed like a goat's symbolized the stability of the earth. The horns on his head were like the rays of the sun and the horns of the moon. As he played his seven-reed pipe, which echoed the seven harmonious sounds of heaven, he wore a fawn skin with spots like the stars in the sky. Although those who passed through the woods at night were sometimes frightened by the wild noises he made (giving rise to the word "panic"), the god was actually quite friendly to mortals and was a special friend to shepherds and musicians.

When Jesus was born, according to Luke 2:15-20, the shepherds followed the great star in the sky to the manger where the Holy Infant was born. They fell to their knees to ask for his blessing, and played lullabies on their pipes to send him to sleep.

It is said that night terrible groans were heard in the mountains. It was later assumed to be the cries of Pan as he lay mortally wounded. The Greek writer Plutarch wrote that, at the hour of Christ's death on the cross, mariners heard a cry sweep across the waves. The cry said, "Great Pan is dead!"

The symbolism of the sacred tree evolved slowly over several thousand years; yet, when monotheism became a strong influence, the final transformation was completed in only a few centuries. Jewish leaders and prophets denounced pagan gods and religious practices starting at least 2000 years before Christ, but a significant threat to paganism, in Europe and the Near East, did not appear until the ascent of Christianity.

The early Christians were zealous in their condemnation of pagan practices. This made them none too popular with the Romans, the ruling nation of the day. Despite severe persecution, Christianity gained a stronghold in the Near East and eventually became a major influence. Some of the early attacks on paganism involved the desecration of sacred groves. One wood that suffered this fate was the Grove of Daphne in Syria near Antioch.

The Grove of Daphne

According to myth, Daphne was a nymph who, inspired by the goddess Diana, was determined to remain a virgin and live the life of a huntress in the forest. One day Apollo, smitten by one of Cupid's arrows, approached her in the woods, and Daphne, in fear of the sun god's advances, ran away. With the god chasing after her, just moments away, she called in desperation to her father, the river

god, to help her. He changed her into a laurel, which was ever after known as one of the sacred trees of Apollo.

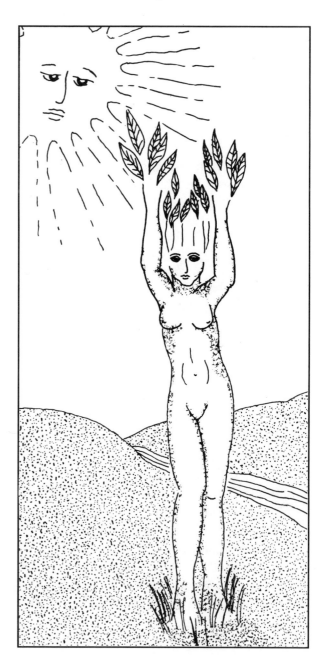

The Grove of Daphne was planted by Seleucus, King of Syria, on the spot where the miraculous transformation was thought to have taken place. It was ten miles in circumference and consisted of avenues of laurel and cypress trees leading to a glorious temple dedicated to Apollo and Diana in the center. An enormous statue of Apollo stood inside. The sacred grounds and temple became well-known for their beauty and splendor. Numerous pilgrims to the area added their own decorations. Eventually a village named Daphne was built to accommodate the hordes of visitors who, for centuries, came to celebrate health, happiness and love.

When Christianity became popular, the people of Syria started to abandon the ancient rites. The Romans, who occupied the land at the time, were unhappy with the rising power of the Christians and tried to force them to convert to paganism.

The Roman emperor Decius appointed a day, known in Christian literature as the Persecution of Decius, upon which all those whose religious allegiance was doubtful were brought before a local commission. Each suspect was forced to offer a sacrifice to the old Roman gods, make a declaration denouncing Christ and Christianity, and participate in a formal banquet where the wines and foods used in the sacrifice were consumed. Those who refused were put to death or tortured until they gave in.

During the Persecution of Decius a bishop from Antioch named Babylas was killed. His distraught congregation brought his remains into the center of the Grove of Daphne and erected a church in his honor.

Years later, when the last pagan Roman emperor, Julian the Apostate, attempted to reinstate the rites of Apollo, the sanctuary was torn down and the body removed. Julian was not trying to destroy Christianity. His plan was to encourage paganism to grow without creating more Christian martyrs. Al-

though he had a special interest in paganism, he hoped to create a society where all religions could flourish side by side.

After trying for years to re-establish the old religion at Daphne without success, he finally allowed the remains of Babylas to be returned to the grove. They were accompanied by a lengthy procession of Christian worshipers who chanted triumphant psalms against idols and idolators. In the course of the evening the pagan temple was set afire and the statue of Apollo was destroyed. Afterwards Julian angrily blamed the Christians for the destruction, while the Christians attributed it to the holy and justified wrath of God.

Converting the Pagans

During its first 300 years, the Church in Rome maintained a staunch position against all pagan beliefs and practices; however, many new and potential converts were reluctant to give up their familiar celebrations. One of the most popular holidays in the Roman year was the Saturnalia. It was a week-long festival with torchlight processions, gift-giving and merry-making, culminating in a winter solstice feast on

Yuletide merry-makers.

December 25, called *Natilis Solis Invicti* or The Birthday of the Unconquerable Sun. The holiday honored the strength of the sun and the fertility it would soon bring to the earth.

In 375 A.D. the Church announced that the birth date of Christ had been discovered to be December 25, and allowed some of the light-hearted customs of the older celebration, such as feasting, dancing and the exchange of gifts, to be incorporated into the reverent observance of Christmas. The use of greenery, however, popularly used to decorate homes and holy places during the Saturnalia, was still prohibited as pagan idolatry.

Over the next 500 years Christianity was introduced in France, England, and Germany. During the conversion process, the Church felt compelled to attack all vestiges of paganism as if on a battlefield and, in the carnage, sacred trees and groves literally came under the axe. The early church councils railed against tree worship and one, the Council of Nantes, specifically commanded the destruction of "divine trees." The righteous enthusiasm with which the priests went about their task was both horrifying and compelling to the native people and became the subject of many a legend.

King Canute forbade the cele-

Early Christian woodcutters who took down sacred trees and groves.

bration of any ceremony connected with pagan worship of any kind. The old pagan gods and goddesses were described as devils, and it was pronounced a sin to even say their names. Attempts to retain the old myths and stories suffered as the Catholic priesthood took on the job of reinterpreting them for the masses. Official polytheistic religions were abandoned with relative speed; but,

even where people admired the power of the Church, the older earth-oriented traditions were not so easily eradicated.

In many communities where the populace gave up the old gods and mythologies, the priests were stopped from hurting the sacred trees. For example, St. Martin was allowed to destroy a pagan temple in the diocese of Tours but not the sacred pine which stood beside it. In response to his insistence that the tree was not a true deity and was, therefore, abhorrent to God, the people asked that he prove it by letting the tall evergreen fall on his head when it was cut. The tree was left alone and, in similar cases, the Church was forced to use other methods of conversion.

When a sacred tree or grove could not be destroyed, churches were often built in the midst of them. In Ireland, St. Patrick's church at Armagh and St. Bridget's church at Kildare were built near sacred oak trees. Kildare, in fact, means "church of the oak." This was done purposely so that, in time, the congregation would transfer its devotion from the trees to the church beside them, just as they had rejected the old goddesses and gods for the new One God.

In a few generations, the people learned to think of churches as sanctuaries and the magical, holy woods as evil, dark places haunted by witches and demons. In the Middle Ages the Grove of Odin, once the scene of numerous animal and human sacrifices done in the belief of their holy significance, became known for that same reason as "the fearsome Brocken." Odin became Satan and his faithful maidens, the Valkyries, were redefined as witches.

Chapel Oak of Allouville, Normandy

Witches concocting an ointment to be used for flying to the Sabbath. By Hans Baldung Grien, Strassburg, 1514.

Certain popular holidays, such as Yule, and customs such as lighting candles and offering small sacrifices under certain holy trees could not be easily suppressed, so they were given new meanings. Yuletide rituals were incorporated into Christmas. The candles were lit to remember Christ as light of the world. The holy offerings came to symbolize the gifts the wise men brought.

In some parts of Europe even today, small crucifixes and images of the Virgin Mary can be found in what used to be ancient sacred forests, affixed to the trunks of trees or hung from the branches. Taking the place of images of the old gods and goddesses, these Christian symbols are used to drive away the tree demons—the ancient deities—who hide under the bark.

As the more gradual method of conversion proved to be successful the Christians relaxed. By the time missionaries reached the Scandinavian countries in the tenth and eleventh centuries, they had learned to be more tolerant of native customs. They no longer feared the ancient gods and used the full range of popular mythology to their advantage.

Norse mythology taught that the great gods were destined to die. When the Catholic priesthood came into power, they proclaimed that the old gods were dead and that the one all-powerful God had come to bring the people everlasting salvation. There was no need for them to destroy the groves or transform the old deities into devils. Instead, the old laws, stories and celebrations were joyously kept and carefully assimilated with the new. In this manner the folk could honor the sacred memory of the old religion yet happily embrace the new one without too much conflict. New symbolism for old customs was adopted much more quickly and peacefully and, although the Church still opposed pagan symbols and practices and occasionally reverted to its earlier methods of suppression, it had learned a valuable lesson.

Why Evergreens Are Green
Cherokee tribe, North America

Manitou, the Great Mystery, and O-kee, the Evil One, were brothers who fought constantly. Now Manitou was the stronger of the two. When their arguments at last ceased O-kee went to dwell in the canyons where he plotted to overthrow Manitou, with the help of unhappy spirits he forced to serve him.

Manitou planted a beautiful forest in which he planned to put peaceful and happy beings. O-kee darted through the dark clouds and his wicked laughter echoed in thunder.

The Great Mystery planted flowers and other beautiful plants. In the darkness O-kee came and touched the stems leaving thorns. At dawn there could be seen teardrops on the sorrowing flower petals.

Birds of fantastic plumage and all manner of animals lived in the forest. Fish and turtles and frogs and many other creatures lived in the water. Spirits danced among the waterfalls and dwelt in the mountains and glades. But mankind was not yet created.

O-kee went to Manitou with a handful of leaves as his contribution for human beings. "Oak leaves will make strong warriors. Maple leaves will curl gracefully on the waters and be good fishermen. Women will be tall and graceful like poplar leaves."

Manitou accepted O-kee's gift. He peopled the earth with leaf men and leaf women. But they were like withered leaves, frail in mind and body, never satisfied or content. Their hearts changed with every gust of thought.

The Great Mystery called these people to offer a tribute of gratitude. Many were weak, wicked and ungrateful. But some did send up their gratitude. The dogwoods, the alders, the maples and the poplars shed their leaves in amber and flame for all they owed the creator. The mountains and valleys were like a rainbow as sumac, sassafras, purple aster, goldenrod, pleurisy weed, mullein and bittersweet offered their banners of red, yellow, purple, ochre and brown.

But O-kee poisoned the pines, hemlocks, spruces, firs and cedars with evil thoughts. "We owe you nothing, Manitou. Why should we shed a single needle? We have weathered and battled alone and owe nothing to anyone."

They stood aloof, distant from their cousins, the other trees and plants. But after the pines saw the beauty of the sacrifice made by the others, they felt sorry for their selfishness. They cried out, "We, too, will give up our needles if streaks of yellow and red will brighten our branches and fall to earth like molting feathers."

But it was too late. The Great Sky Father hears only the prayers of a willing heart.

When the winter winds pass them by the evergreens cry out in their dreary dark green robes, but they are not heard. The arrogant pines never know the glory their brother trees know.

The Thunder Oak
Germany

At the time the people of the city of Geismar in the landgraviate of Hesse still worshipped the old gods, there grew a giant tree, branching with huge limbs toward the clouds. It was known as the Thunder Oak, sacred to the god Thor.

In the dead of night, Thor's priests brought sacrifices of both beasts and men to the altar of the thunder god. The blood of the sacrifices watered the roots of the tree and mistletoe sprang from its branches. It was so terrible a spot that no beasts or birds rested within the branches of this tree, or in its shade.

One Christmas Eve, Thor's priests held their winter rites beneath the Thunder Oak. The townsfolk trudged through the deep snow bent on keeping their sacred feast.

When they had all gathered, and the priests were just raising their knives to slay their human victims, the good Saint Wynfred hurried to the altar. He swiftly drew an axe from his girdle and smote the mighty oak, hewing a deep gash in its trunk. He swung again and again as the worshippers gazed in horror.

Suddenly a mighty rush of wind blasted into the tree, causing it to fall to the ground with a tremendous crash. It split into four pieces. Just behind it, completely unharmed, stood a tiny young fir tree.

Saint Wynfred dropped his axe and turned to speak. "This little tree shall be your holy tree tonight. It is the tree of peace and salvation, a tree of life, a tree of hope. Behold, how it points toward heaven! Let this tree be called the Tree of the Christ Child. Gather about it, not in the wildwood, but in your homes. There it will shelter no bloody deeds, just loving gifts and acts of kindness. Let the peace of Christ reign in your hearts!"

The people took the little fir to the house of their chief and celebrated around it. They later learned the rites of Christmas in the chapel of Saint Peter which Saint Wynfred built of the wood of the Thunder Oak.

The Old Pine Is Blessed
unknown origin

When King Herod's law forced Joseph, Mary and the Christ Child to flee, they one night had to sleep in the middle of a forest. They crept inside an old hollow pine tree which lowered its branches to conceal them until Herod's soldiers passed.

When morning came the Christ child raised his arms and blessed the old pine. It is said that if you cut a small pine cone lengthwise you can still see the imprint of his hand.

The Singing Fir Tree
Switzerland

There once was a master woodcarver who lived in the village of Reckingen in the canton of Valais. Many of the churches in this region were beautified by his special handiwork, which was the carving of sacred figures of the saints, and church pews decorated with wooden foliage.

One evening when the church bell of Reckingen rang for the hour of prayer the woodcarver heard strange but beautiful singing. He went to his window to listen and noticed it seemed to be coming from the forest of Hohbach which covered the steep hills that rose above the village.

The singing stopped as soon as the bell stopped ringing. "My imagination is running away with me," the woodcarver muttered to himself as he put away his tools and hurried to church. But the next night he heard the singing again. And the night after that he heard it once more. In fact, the strange music began every time the church bell rang for evening prayers and ended when the bell stopped ringing every night for the next several nights. The woodcarver was understandably relieved to discover that many other villagers heard it as well.

One evening during prayer time, he climbed the hill to the forest of Hohbach determined to find the source of the mysterious music. He wandered about among the huge trees for a long time. At last the singing led him to a giant fir hundreds of years old. To his astonishment the sound seemed to come from out of its trunk! When it was again quiet he ran to the village to report his discovery. After that, each evening several of his neighbors climbed the hill to the miraculous tree and stood in reverent amazement beside it.

The woodcarver visited the tree often and ran his hands across its bark. The giant fir was constantly in his thoughts, even appearing in his dreams. He became obsessed with the idea of making a carving out of it, to be the most magnificent work he had ever done.

The parish finally agreed to cut down the tree and let him work on it. But the woodcutters harbored a secret misgiving as they felled the magnificent fir, and their hearts grew heavy as they dragged it down to the valley with horses.

The master carver cut himself a huge block from the heart of the tree. He told the parish he was going to make a statue of the Virgin Mary and set to work that very night. He toiled day in and day out and in his zeal almost forgot to eat. People flocked from miles away to watch the Holy Mother slowly emerge from the wood. The woodcarver was truly talented and his work a veritable masterpiece. All said that no artist had ever made Mary look so beautiful and alive.

When the statue was finished it was presented to the church of Reckingen. The priest took the statue and placed it on the alter as the people watched in silent awe. Then suddenly the wooden figure of Mary opened its mouth, and once more the familiar dulcet tones of the miraculous music were heard.

That was the last time the fir tree sang.

Silver Fir Cones
Hartz Mountains, Germany

Once upon a time a miner who had a wife and seven children was confined to his bed with a terrible illness. They were a poor family. As days went by and the man did not recover, there was soon no meat in the cupboard nor fire on the hearth.

The miner's wife was getting desperate and finally told her husband that she would go into the woods on the hill of Hubinchenstein to gather fir cones. "With some fir cones I could make a fire and perhaps I could sell the others to buy meat," she said.

She took a large basket and climbed the hill into the deep dark forest. As she walked and gathered she thought about her troubles until at last they overcame her. She sat down on a tree stump weeping.

"What is the matter with you and why are you stealing my fir cones?" said a voice right beside her.

The woman jumped up with fright and saw a frowning dwarf with a long white beard standing before her. She fell to her knees to beg forgiveness and blurted out her sad story.

The dwarf's expression softened with kindness. "Please get up, my good woman. Troubles come to us all. But you must leave these fir cones here as they belong to me. Go into the next forest. The fir cones you pick up over there will suit you much better."

So the woman replaced the fir cones she had gathered and went to the next forest as the dwarf had instructed. It was a long way. By time she got there she was very tired and needed to set her basket down to rest a bit. As soon as she did fir cones fell like hail out of the trees and filled her basket.

She was frightened and ran home as fast as she could. On the way the basket grew heavier and heavier until, just as she reached her door, she could hold on to it no longer. She dropped it, spilling its contents on the ground.

Then she saw why the basket was so heavy. Every one of the fir cones had turned to silver.

At first she thought the little man must have been Satan, but after talking with her husband she realized he was Gubich, King of the Dwarfs and helper of the poor. She went into town and sold some of the fir cones and returned with everything her family needed. Although her husband was sick and could not eat they all went to bed with happy hearts.

The next day the woman went back into the forest. She found Gubich near the same tree stump and poured out her thanks to him. "Thank me no thanks, my good woman!" he laughed. "I am happy to be of service."

He stooped to pick a plant from the ground and gave it to her. "Take this home and strip it of its leaves. Put the leaves in a pot and boil them. When the water turns green give it to your husband to drink." And then he disappeared.

The woman was still a little afraid to follow the dwarf's advice. "What if he really is Satan? This might be poison," she thought. But when she returned home her husband was worse and seemed close to death. "I must trust that the dwarf is good."

She boiled the leaves of the plant into a green tea and gave it to her husband to drink. Almost immediately color came back to his cheeks and strength flowed through his body. He leaped out of bed a well man.

They had enough fir cones to never want again in times of trouble. They never saw Gubich again but thanked him in their hearts daily and kept one of the silver fir cones on the dresser to remember him by. The children kept the silver cone when they were older and their children kept it after them.

The people of the same region of the Hartz Mountains keep a silver fir cone on their dressers to this day as a reminder of the kindness of Gubich, the King of the Dwarfs.

"Redemption from the Fall of Man," by Giovanni da Modena.

CHAPTER SEVEN

Rebirth of the Tree

The tree casts its shade upon all, even upon the wood-cutter.
—SANSKRIT PROVERB

O Christmas Tree! Fair Christmas Tree!
A type of life eternal!
O Christmas Tree! Fair Christmas Tree!
Your boughs are ever vernal.
So fresh and green in summer heat,
And bright when snows lie round your feet.
O Christmas Tree! Fair Christmas Tree!
A type of life eternal!
—GERMAN CHRISTMAS CAROL

The Tree of the Cross

In the Middle Ages the story of Christ, which already fit the tradition of the dying god, was more obviously connected to the important concept of the Tree of Life. A popular legend sprung up that told how the seed of the Tree of Life grew up to be the very tree which served as Christ's cross. Early representations of Jesus actually show him crucified in a flowering tree. The cross became yet another symbol of the center.

Just as the Tree of Life was the passageway between planes of existence that allowed a return to life, the cross was the passageway of salvation, the ladder by means of which the soul could reach God. According to Christian dogma, Christ suffered on this new tree so that the eternal life taken from humanity by the sin of Adam and Eve could be restored.

This change in the meaning of the center was far from subtle as it broke with the notion of an eternal cycle. Jesus' death and revival occurred once, not every year. The salvation it promised would happen once for eternity, not over and over again. It is hard to say what this shift from a cyclical to a linear world view has meant to our culture. A guess is that it

The Dear Old Tree

BY LUELLA WILSON SMITH

There's a
dear old tree,
an evergreen
tree,
And it blossoms
once a year.
'Tis loaded
with fruit from
top to root,
And it brings to
all good cheer.

For it's blossoms
bright are small
candles white
And it's fruit is
dolls and toys,
And they all are
free for both
you and me
If we're good little
girls & boys.

either reflected or helped complete the process of human alienation from nature, encouraging the need for a paternalistic savior.

Adam and Eve Day

The Church furthered the assimilation of this new concept when it allowed the day before Christmas to be devoted to the memory of Adam and Eve. Adam and Eve were commemorated as saints in the calendars of the Greek Orthodox and other Eastern churches. Their veneration spread to the West and became popular toward the end of the first millennium. The Roman Catholic Church never *officially* introduced the day, but statues of the "first parents" can still be found among images of the saints in many old churches in Europe.

Since most people could not read, important stories were dramatized at the appropriate time of year by individual storytellers or acting troupes. It was only natural that the play telling the story of the Creation and Fall became popularly connected with that of the Nativity. The story of Adam and Eve usually ended with the promise of the coming Savior. This came from Genesis 3:15, which was interpreted in the Middle Ages as foretelling the coming of Christ. The play thus led directly into the Story of Bethlehem.

In Germany these plays were known as the Paradise Plays. They were performed in the open on large squares in front of churches, or inside the church. The only prop used was a variation of the old symbol for the Yggdrasil or Yule Tree, an evergreen fir hung with apples. In this instance it represented both the Tree of Life and the Tree of Knowledge in the Garden of Eden. When the play was performed in the church, the *paradeisbaum* (tree of paradise) was surrounded by lighted candles and the action took place inside the ring.

The Christmas Tree

Centuries later, after the Church suppressed mystery plays due to the coarse language and jokes the actors had begun adding to please the crowd, the Paradise Tree found its way into Christian homes. It symbolized the coming savior and often stood beside the Yule Tree, which symbolized eternal life. Since the symbolism of the two was connected, it seems likely that eventually people began to use one tree to take the place of both.

Illustration by Ludwig Richter, c. 1803

The original Yule Tree was a living evergreen planted in a tub and brought indoors. It was not decorated. It is not clear from the records whether the Paradise Tree was living or cut; but it is apparent that when the meaning of the solstice-season tree became increasingly more blurred, the use of a living tree faded away.

The use of decorations on the tree varies considerably from place to place. Each family developed its own customs but there were some general trends. At first the main decorations were the apples from the Paradise Tree. In the fifteenth century, small white wafers representing the Holy Eucharist were added. These were later replaced with pastries cut in the shape of stars, angels, hearts, flowers and bells.

The tree was also decorated with garlands of real or paper roses. This custom comes from a legend about trees that bloomed on the night of Christ's birth. The most famous of these is that of the Glastonbury Thorn.

According to the legend, when St. Joseph of Arimathea came to Glastonbury, England, he planted his staff into the earth and it sprouted leaves. After that it blossomed every Christmas Eve. Trees of the same species, a type of hawthorn, adopted the same habit throughout England.

This story almost certainly came from an earlier legend about trees which bloomed at Yule. The old German Yule was a one-to-two month nonstop feast which began early in November. Occasionally mild weather in November encouraged the trees to bloom. The rarity of this phenomenon gave rise to the legends which the church adopted for its own.

There were stories told about celebrated pagan magicians who made summer in the heart of winter. These stories were later incorporated by Catholic monks into stories of the lives of certain saints. The idea of trees blooming and bearing fruit in the unusual summer was attributed to the power of Christ.

One popular story told how the Fir Tree of Life once bloomed and fruited year round. One day Eve plucked one of its fruits causing all its fruit and flowers to drop off and its foliage to shrivel up into tiny needle-like leaves. It never bloomed again until the night Christ was born.

"Hoisting the Union Jack," by Alfred Hunt. From Illustrated London News, *Dec. 1876.*

Up to the middle of the seventeenth century, the Christbaum (as it was now called) had no lights. Candles were placed on a pyramid, called the lichtstock, made of graduated wooden shelves. Although the lichtstock is still used in parts of Germany, the candles eventually found their way onto the tree.

There are several stories about the origin of the custom of using lights on the trees. In the Middle Ages the idea of a light-bearing tree was very popular. An Icelandic legend, well-known at the time, relates that once upon a time there stood a mountain ash that sprung from the blood of two innocent people who were executed. Every Christmas Eve the tree was covered with lights that the strongest gale could not blow out.

The most well-known story about lights on the tree attributes their introduction to Martin Luther, leader of the Reformation movement in the sixteenth century (see stories that follow this chapter). This is significant because it shows that the Protestant reformers needed a way to justify the continued use of the tree even while they were rejecting other aspects of basic Catholic theology.

So developed the Christmas Tree, with the ornaments, colored lights and pastries that we know today. From Germany the custom was brought to England where it was popularized by Prince Albert, consort to Queen Victoria. By this time the tree had taken on room-size proportions, making it impossible to use a living tree even if the idea still existed. Soon afterwards German immigrants brought the custom to America, where

it spread and quickly became one of the most popular Christmas traditions. Except for the substitution of electric lights for candles, the tree has changed very little from the time it was first introduced in this country.

The Christmas Tree is not just a pretty thing to look at. It has a special place in the spiritual history of us all and, since its ancient symbolism is embedded in our familiar modern religions, it still has the power to stir us deep in our primal souls.

"Martin Luther," from Matthews Onidius' Dialogi, *1521.*

The original winter solstice holiday was a joyous celebration of the cycle of nature—a reaffirmation of the continuation of life and renewal of humankind's intimate relationship with all the universe. The tree makes an outstanding symbol for all these values. It is shorthand for our human connection with the great, exuberant cycles of life.

There is nothing in these general values that is contradictory to the spirit of Christmas as it is now celebrated. With the additional trappings of Christian symbolism it makes a lovely image for Christmas; yet the enjoyment of the evergreen need not be restricted to Christian worshippers. Although few would advocate a complete return to the pagan rites with the bloodshed that sometimes entailed, new rituals with emphasis on ancient symbolism are becoming more popular.

Since the tree is a product of nature, dressed in its solstice finery it still glorifies and reaffirms our connection to the earth. As such it seems fitting that many people have begun to revive the custom of using a live evergreen for their celebration. The tree can be planted in the forest or in yards with the return of spring. We need to remember our symbiotic relationship with nature so we can preserve and enjoy the earth for many Christmases to come.

The Legend of the True Cross
popular throughout Europe in the Middle Ages

After Adam was banished from the Garden of Eden he lived a long life filled with toil and penitence. When his years were nearly over, he instructed his son Seth to ask the Archangel in the Garden of Eden for a balsam from the Tree of Life to save him from death. "You will need no directions to find your way to the Garden as my footsteps scorched the soil as I left."

Seth left immediately. As he drew near the garden he saw the flaming sword in the hand of the Archangel who stood with wings outspread to block the entrance. Seth fell to his knees and covered his face, unable to say a word. "The time of pardon will not come for another four thousand years," said the Archangel. "Then the Redeemer will reopen the gate to Adam and his offspring. But as a token of future salvation, the wood on which redemption shall be won shall grow from your father's tomb."

The Archangel swung open the huge gate of gold and fire so Seth could look inside. He saw a crystal-clear fountain gushing forth in four flowing streams. Before it grew a magnificent evergreen tree with a massive trunk. A great serpent coiled around its base scorching the bark with its breath and devouring its leaves. Beneath the tree was the pit which leads to hell. The branches of the tree reached to heaven. They were covered with green leaves, flowers and fruit. At the top of the tree was a small baby who glowed like the sun and whose head was encircled by seven sweetly-singing white doves. A most radiant woman held the child in her arms. "This is the Tree of Life," said the Archangel as he took three seeds from it and handed them to Seth. "When Adam is dead place these seeds in his mouth and bury him."

Seth left with the seeds and did as he was told. Three trees—a cedar, a cypress and a pine—grew from his father's grave. They intertwined as they grew and eventually became one trunk. It was beneath this tree that King David sat and repented for his sins.

In the time of King Solomon this was the noblest of the trees in Lebanon. When Solomon built his palace, he cut down the tree to make a pillar to support the roof. But the tree refused to be used for such a purpose. It sometimes appeared too long and sometimes too short. When the palace walls were lowered to fit the pillar it shot up and pierced the roof. The angry king had the tree thrown across the brook Cedron so that people would trample on it as they crossed.

The Queen of Sheba recognized its sacred qualities, however, and persuaded Solomon to bury it instead. Some time passed, and the king dug the pool of Bethesda at the very same spot. The pool acquired miraculous properties because of the tree that lay beneath.

Close to the time of Christ's crucifixion the wood rose to the surface and was brought out. It was used to make his cross.

Lot and the Tree of the Cross
Palestine

Before the great patriarch Abraham died, he gave three seedlings to Lot, who planted them where the Convent of the Cross near Jerusalem now stands. The young plants appeared healthy; yet, try as he might, Lot could not get them to grow. This was because they needed to be watered by a righteous man, and Lot had fallen into sin.

One day an angel came down from heaven to warn Lot that unless the shoots entrusted to him grew he could not be saved. "These plants must flourish, Lot," said the angel. "To make sure that they do, you must fetch water from the River Jordan for them."

So Lot saddled up his donkey and rode down into the valley to get the water. On his return he passed by the Inn of the Good Samaritan where a pilgrim stopped him and begged for a drink. Lot gave his water skin to the man who proceeded to drink it dry.

There was nothing Lot could do but go back to the river and bring water up again. But once more, along the road home, Lot met a pilgrim who asked for a drink. He, too, was so thirsty that he drank all the water and forced Lot to return to the river. This series of events happened a third time; by then Lot was in despair.

When Lot cried out in frustration and grief the angel appeared. "Do not despair," the angel said. "You have done well. The pilgrim was really the Evil One in disguise who came to tempt you. Since you have passed this test you may now fulfill your duty by watering the plants. Go!"

So Lot returned home and watered the shoots. As he watched they quickly began to grow, twisting around each other, until they became one full-grown tree made of three kinds—cedar, cypress and pine. Many centuries later the wood from this magnificent tree was used for the cross upon which Jesus was crucified.

Martin Luther and the First Christmas Tree
Germany

One clear cold Christmas Eve the famous Reformation leader Martin Luther was walking home through the woods. As it was a beautiful starry night, he paused for a moment to gaze at the sky in reverent meditation. He was in a grove of tall pines. Their fragrance reminded him of incense and the peaceful murmur of the wind in their branches sounded like a congregation at prayer. From where he stood it seemed as though the thousands of stars had settled on their branches.

He proceeded to cut a tiny tree and took it home where he decorated it with small candles in metal holders to recreate his experience for his children. That glittering tree became a tradition for his family in the many Christmases to come just as it has for many other families around the world.

The Little Stranger
Germany

Once upon a time a poor woodcutter lived with his wife and two children in a small cottage on the border of a great forest. The children's names were Valentine and Mary. They were very good and rose early every morning to help their mother with chores. Their father toiled long hours every day, but his labor produced barely enough money for them to survive.

One winter night they sat about the fire listening to a fierce storm raging outside. The wind howled and their windows rattled with every mighty blast. Even though their stomachs were not full, they were happy to be together inside where it was safe and warm. When the storm was at its worst they answered a knock at the door. A small child stood there, shivering and dressed in rags. "May I stay with you tonight?" he asked. "I have nothing to eat and no place to go."

The woodcutter's wife wrapped a blanket around his tiny shoulders as she brought the little stranger inside. "Of course, come in, come in. How could we allow you to stay outside on a night like this? We do not have much food but you may have what there is, and you may sleep with the children in their warm bed." The child's face brightened and, after eating a few morsels of food, he fell sound asleep.

When Valentine and Mary said their evening prayers they thanked God for their richness. Whereas the little visitor had only heaven for a roof and the cold earth for a bed, they had loving parents and a warm home. They fell asleep with thankful hearts.

In the middle of the night Mary was awakened by beautiful singing and woke her brother so he could hear it too. They ran to look out their window and saw the child standing in the snow with a throng of angels singing. He was no longer in rags but in glittering robes. A halo ringed his lovely head and peace and love radiated from his being. "I am the Christ child who brings happiness to good children. I bring you a blessing. This little fir tree which stands outside your window shall be my emblem." The fir was then miraculously covered in silver nuts, lights, apples and threads of gold, becoming the Christbaum or Christmas Tree we know today.

The Little Fir at Bethlehem
Sicily

On the night of Christ's birth, living creatures from far and wide journeyed to the stable in Bethlehem to honor the newborn King and bring him gifts.

Even the trees of the forest came. The olive gave its fruit. The palm brought its dates. Every tree had something to offer except the tiny fir. It came a long distance and was so weary it could barely stand. Then the larger trees pushed it into the background where it could not be seen.

A nearby angel felt sorry for the sad little tree. He went to the stars and asked some of them to come down and rest in its branches. The stars obeyed and shone there like candles. When Baby Jesus saw the lovely sight, his heart filled with gladness and he smiled. He blessed the happy little tree and declared that fir trees should evermore be decorated and lit up to warm the hearts of children at Christmas time.

The Fir Tree

a fairy tale by Hans Christian Andersen, Denmark

Out in the forest stood a pretty little Fir Tree. It had a good place; it could have sunlight, air there was in plenty, and all around grew many larger comrades—pines as well as firs. But the little Fir Tree wished ardently to become greater. It did not care for the warm sun and the fresh air; it took no notice of the peasant children, who went about talking together, when they had come out to look for strawberries and raspberries. Often they came with a whole potful, or had strung berries on a straw; then they would sit down by the little Fir Tree and say, "How pretty and small that one is!" and the Tree did not like to hear that at all.

Next year it had grown a great joint, and the following year it was longer still, for in fir trees one can always tell by the number of rings they have how many years they have been growing.

"Oh, if I were only as great a tree as the others!" sighed the little Fir, "then I would spread my branches far around, and look out from my crown into the wide world. The birds would then build nests in my boughs, and when the wind blew I could nod just as grandly as the others yonder."

It took no pleasure in the sunshine, in the birds, and in the red clouds that went sailing over it morning and evening. When it was winter, and the snow lay all around, white and sparkling, a hare would often come jumping along, and spring right over the little Fir Tree. Oh! This made it so angry. But two winters went by, and when the third came, the little Tree had grown so tall that the hare was obliged to run around it.

"Oh! To grow, to grow, and become old; that's the only fine thing in the world," thought the Tree.

In the autumn woodcutters always came and felled a few of the largest trees. The little Fir Tree, that was now quite well grown, shuddered with fear, for the great stately trees fell to the ground with a crash, and their branches were cut off, so that the trees looked quite naked, long, and slender. In fact, they could hardly be recognized. But then they were laid upon wagons, and horses dragged them away out of the wood. Where were they going? What destiny awaited them?

In the spring, when the Swallows and the Stork came, the Tree asked them, "Do you know where they were taken? Did you not meet them?"

The Swallows knew nothing about it, but the Stork looked thoughtful, nodded his head, and said:

"Yes, I think so. I met many new ships when I flew out of Egypt; on the ships were stately masts; I fancy that these were the trees. They smelt like fir. I can assure you they're stately, very stately."

"Oh that I were only big enough to go over the sea! What kind of thing is this sea, and how does it look?"

"It would take too long to explain all that," said the Stork, and he went away.

"Rejoice in thy youth," said the Sunbeams; "Rejoice in thy fresh growth and in the young life that is within thee."

And the wind kissed the Tree, and the dew wept tears upon it; but the Fir Tree did not understand that.

When Christmas time approached, quite young trees were felled—sometimes trees which were neither so old nor so large as this Fir Tree that never rested but always wanted to go away. These young trees, which were almost the most beautiful, kept all their branches; they were put upon wagons, and horses dragged them away out of the wood.

"Where are they all going?" asked the Fir Tree. "They are not greater than I; indeed one of them was much smaller. Why do they keep all their branches? Whither are they taken?"

"We know that! We know that!" chirped the Sparrows. "Yonder in the town we looked in at the windows. We know where they go. Oh!

They are dressed up in the greatest pomp and splendor that can be imagined. We have looked in at the windows and have perceived that they are planted in the middle of the warm room and adorned with the most beautiful things—gilt apples, honey cakes, playthings, and many hundreds of candles."

"And then?" asked the Fir Tree and trembled through all its branches. "And then? What happens then?"

"Why, we have not seen anything more. But it was incomparable."

"Perhaps I may be destined to tread this glorious path one day!" cried the Fir Tree rejoicingly. "That is even better than traveling across the sea. How painfully I long for it! If it were only Christmas now! Now I am great and grown up, like the rest who were led away last year. Oh, if I were only on the carriage! If I were only in the warm room, among all the pomp and splendor! And then? Yes, then something even better will come, something far more charming, or else why should they adorn me so? There must be something grander, something greater still to come; but what? Oh! I'm suffering, I'm longing! I don't know myself what is the matter with me!"

"Rejoice in us," said Air and Sunshine. "Rejoice in thy fresh youth here in the woodland."

The Fir Tree did not rejoice at all, but it grew and grew; winter and summer it stood there—green, dark green. The people who saw it said, "That's a handsome tree!" and at Christmas time it was felled before any one of the others. The axe cut deep into its marrow, and the tree fell to the ground with a sigh. It felt a pain, a sensation of faintness, and could not think at all of happiness, for it was sad at parting from its home, from the place where it had grown up. It knew that it should never again see the dear old companions, the little bushes and flowers all around, perhaps not even the birds. The parting was not at all agreeable.

The Tree only came to itself when it was unloaded in a yard with the other trees and heard a man say:

"This one is famous; we only want this one!"

Now two servants came in gay liveries, and carried the Fir Tree into a large beautiful salon. All around the walls hung pictures, and by the great stove stood large Chinese vases with lions on the covers; there were rocking chairs, silken sofas; great tables covered with picture books, and toys worth a hundred times a hundred dollars, at least the children said so. And the Fir Tree was put into a great tub filled with sand; but no one could see that it was a tub, for it was hung round with green cloth, and stood on a large many-colored carpet. Oh, how the Tree trembled! What was to happen now? The servants, and the young ladies also, decked it out. On one branch they hung little nets, cut out of colored paper; every net was filled with sweetmeats; golden apples and

An illustration from The Fir Tree *by Hans Christian Andersen, 1850.*

walnuts hung down as if they grew there, and more than a hundred little candles in red, white, and blue were fastened to the different boughs. Dolls that looked exactly like real people—the Tree had never seen such before—swung among the foliage, and high on the summit of the Tree was fixed a tinsel star. It was splendid, particularly splendid.

"This evening," said all, "this evening it will shine."

"Oh," thought the Tree, "that it were evening already! Oh, that the lights may be soon lit up! When may that be done? Will the sparrows fly against the panes? Shall I grow fast here, and stand adorned in summer and winter?"

Yes, he did not guess badly. But he had a complete backache from mere longing, and the backache is just as bad for a Tree as the headache for a person.

At last the candles were lighted. What a brilliance, what splendor! The Tree trembled so in all its branches that one of the candles set fire to a green twig, and it was scorched.

"Heaven preserve us!" cried the young ladies; and they hastily put the fire out.

Now the Tree might not even tremble. Oh, that was terrible! It was so afraid of setting fire to some of its ornaments, and it was quite bewildered with all the brilliance. And now the folding doors were thrown open, and a number of children rushed in as if they would have overturned the whole Tree; the older people followed more deliberately. The little ones stood quite silent, but only for a minute; then they shouted till the room rang. They danced gleefully round the Tree, and one present after another was plucked from it.

"What are they about?" thought the Tree. "What's going to be done?"

The candles burned down to the twigs, and as they burned down they were extinguished, and then the children received permission to plunder the Tree. Oh! They rushed in upon it so that every branch cracked again. If it had not been fastened by the top and by the golden star to the ceiling, it would have fallen down.

The children danced about with their pretty toys. No one looked at the Tree except one old man, who came up and peeped among the branches, but only to see if a fig or an apple had not been forgotten.

"A story! a story!" shouted the children. They drew a little fat man toward the Tree. He sat down just beneath it, "for then we shall be in the green wood," said he, "and the tree may have the advantage of listening to my tale. But I can only tell one. Will you hear the story of Ivede-Avede, or of Klumpey-Dumpey, who fell downstairs and still was raised up to honor and married the Princess?"

"Ivede-Avede!" cried some, "Klumpey-Dumpey!" cried others, and there was a great crying and shouting. Only the Fir Tree was quite silent, and thought, "Shall I not be in it? Shall I have nothing to do in it?" But it had been in the evening's amusement and had done what was required of it.

Then the fat man told about Klumpey-Dumpey, who fell downstairs and yet was raised to honor and married the Princess. The children clapped their hands and cried, "Tell another! tell another!" for they wanted to hear about Ivede-Avede; but they only got the story of Klumpey-Dumpey. The Fir Tree stood quite silent and thoughtful; never had the birds in the wood told such a story as that. Klumpey-Dumpey fell downstairs and yet came to honor and married the Princess!

"Yes, so it happens in the world!" thought the Fir Tree, and believed it must be true, because that was such a nice man who told it. "Well, who can know? Perhaps I shall fall downstairs too and marry a Princess!" And it looked forward with pleasure to being adorned again the next evening with candles and toys, gold and fruit. "To-morrow I shall not tremble," it thought. "I will rejoice in all my splendor. To-morrow I shall hear the story of Klumpey-Dumpey again, and, perhaps, that of Ivede-Avede too."

The Tree stood all night quiet and thoughtful.

In the morning the servants and the chambermaid came in.

"Now my splendor will begin afresh," thought the Tree. But they dragged it out of the room and upstairs to the garret. Here they put him in a dark corner where no daylight shone.

"What's the meaning of this?" thought the Tree. "What am I to do here? What is to happen?"

The Tree leaned against the wall and thought and thought. And it had time enough, for days and nights went by, and nobody came up; and when at length some one came, it was only to put some great boxes in a corner. Now the Tree stood quite hidden away, and the supposition was that it was quite forgotten.

"Now it's winter outside," thought the Tree. "The earth is hard and covered with snow, and people cannot plant me; therefore, I suppose I'm to be sheltered here until spring comes. How considerate that is! How good people are! If it were only not so dark here and so terribly solitary—not even a little hare! That was pretty out there in the wood, when the snow lay thick and the hare sprang past; yes, even when he jumped over me. Then I did not like it. But it is terribly lonely up here!"

"Piep! piep!" said a little Mouse and crept forward. Then came another little one. They smelt at the Fir Tree and then slipped among the branches.

"It's horribly cold," said the two little Mice, "or else it would be comfortable here. Don't you think so, you old Fir Tree?"

"I'm not old at all," said the Fir Tree. "There are many much older than I."

"Where do you come from?" asked the Mice. "And what do you know?" They were dreadfully inquisitive. "Tell us about the most beautiful spot on earth. Have you been there? Have you been in the storeroom, where the cheeses lie on the shelves and hams hang from the ceiling; where one dances on tallow candles and goes in thin and out fat?"

"I don't know that!" replied the Tree; "but I know the wood, where the sun shines and where the birds sing."

And then it told all about its youth.

And the little Mice had never heard anything of the kind; and they listened and said:

"What a number of things you have seen! How happy you must have been!"

"I?" said the Fir Tree and it thought about what it had told. "Yes, those were really quite happy times." But then it told of the Christmas Eve, when it had been hung with sweetmeats and candles.

"Oh!" said the little Mice, "How happy you have been, you old Fir Tree!"

"I'm not old at all," said the Tree. "I only came out of the wood this winter. I'm only rather backward in my growth."

"What splendid stories you can tell!" said the little Mice.

And next night they came with four other little Mice to hear what the Tree had to relate. The more it said, the more clearly did it remember everything, and thought, "Those were quite merry days! But they may come again. Klumpey-Dumpey fell downstairs and yet he married the Princess. Perhaps I may marry a Princess too!" Then the Fir Tree thought of a pretty little birch tree that grew out in the forest. For the Fir Tree, that birch was a real Princess.

"Who's Klumpey-Dumpey?" asked the little Mice.

Then the Fir Tree told the whole story; it could remember every single word. The little Mice were ready to leap to the very top of the tree with pleasure. Next night a great many more Mice came, and on Sunday two Rats even appeared; but these thought the story was not pretty, and the little Mice were sorry for that. Now they also did not like it so much as before.

"Do you only know one story?" asked the Rats.

"Only that one," replied the Tree. "I heard that on the happiest evening of my life; I did not think then how happy I was."

"That's a very miserable story. Don't you know any about bacon and tallow candles—a storeroom story?"

"No," said the Tree.

"Then we'd rather not hear you," said the Rats.

And they went back to their own people. The little Mice at last stayed away also. Then the Tree sighed and said:

"It was very nice when they sat round me, the merry little Mice, and listened when I spoke to them. Now that's past too. But I shall remember to be pleased when they take me out."

But when did that happen? Why, it was one morning that people came and rummaged in the garret. The boxes were put away and the Tree brought out. They certainly threw it rather roughly on the floor, but a servant dragged it away at once to the stairs, where the daylight shone.

"Now life is beginning again!" thought the Tree.

It felt the fresh air and the first sunbeams, and now it was out in the courtyard. Everything passed so quickly that the Tree quite forgot to look at itself, there was so much to look at all round. The courtyard was close to a garden, and here everything was blooming; the roses hung fresh and fragrant over the little paling, the linden trees were in blossom, and the swallows cried, "Quinze-wit! quinze-wit! my husband's come!" But it was not the Fir Tree that they meant.

"Now I shall live!" said the Tree rejoicingly, and spread its branches far out; but alas! They were all withered and yellow and it lay in the corner among nettles and weeds. The tinsel star was still upon it, and it shone in the bright sunshine.

In the courtyard a couple of the merry children were playing, who had danced round the Tree at Christmas time, and had rejoiced over it. One of the youngest ran up and tore off the golden star.

"Look what is sticking to the ugly old fir tree," said the child, and he trod upon the branches till they cracked again under his boots.

And the Tree looked at all the blooming flowers and the splendor of the garden, and then looked at itself, and wished it had remained in the dark corner of the garret. It thought of its fresh youth in the wood, of the merry Christmas Eve, and of the little Mice which had listened so pleasantly to the story of Klumpey-Dumpey.

"Past! Past!" said the old Tree. "Had I but rejoiced when I could have done so! Past! Past!"

Then the servant came and chopped the Tree into little pieces; a whole bundle lay there. It blazed brightly under the great brewing copper, and it sighed deeply. Each sigh was like a little shot. The children who were at play there ran up and seated themselves at the fire, looked into it, and cried, "Puff! puff!" But at each explosion, which was a deep sigh, the tree thought of a summer day in the woods, or of a winter night there, when the stars beamed. It thought of Christmas Eve and of Klumpey-Dumpey, the only story it had ever heard or knew how to tell. Then the Tree was burned.

The boys played in the garden, and the youngest had on his breast a golden star, which the Tree had worn on its happiest evening. Now that was past, and the Tree's life was past, and the story is past too: past! past!—and that's the way with all stories.

Motifs and Common Themes in Evergreen Stories

The following is a listing of the themes and the stories that contain them:

1. *Everything in nature is alive and imbued with consciousness.*

This concept is the most common one found in fairy tales. It is shown by having plants and animals talk, think and have emotion. Tales that demonstrate this concept include:
Why Some Trees Are Evergreen - Chapter One
When Your Canary Sings - Chapter One
Leelinau - Chapter Two
Rata and the Children of Tane - Chapter Two
The Dancing Brothers - Chapter Five
Why Evergreens Are Green - Chapter Six
The Singing Fir Tree - Chapter Six
The Old Pine Is Blessed - Chapter Six
The Little Fir at Bethlehem - Chapter Seven
The Fir Tree - Chapter Seven

2. *The use of magic.*

The best example of this is in the story called *The Two Pine Cones* in Chapter One. Because the pine cone was a symbol of fertility its special magic was to increase abundance and prosperity of all sorts. As a shaman the wizard had the skill to summon this magic. Rituals and incantations to influence the spirits are mentioned in *Leelinau* and *Rata and the Children of Tane*, both in Chapter Two. Other stories also include the use of magic
The Old Man Who Made Trees Blossom - Chapter Three
Silver Fir Cones - Chapter Six

3. Tree spirits

This motif encompasses both spirits who reside in specific trees and those who reside in the forests. It includes the myriad tales about elves, dwarfs, genii, nymphs, shuralees, etc.
Pitys and Boreas - Chapter One
Leelinau - Chapter Two
The Pine of Akoya - Chapter Two
The Shuralee and the Woodcutter - Chapter Two
Life for a Life - Chapter Two
Rata and the Children of Tane - Chapter Two
The Old Man Who Made Trees Blossom - Chapter Three
Silver Fir Cones - Chapter Six

4. People transformed into trees and trees transformed into people

This theme is related to the idea of the tree as a connector between different forms of existence. It shows up in the following tales:
Pitys and Boreas - Chapter One
The Pine of the Lovers - Chapter Three
The Trees of Faithful Love - Chapter Three
Cyparissus - Chapter Three
The Dancing Brothers - Chapter Five
Ivan Sosnovich - Chapter Five

5. The Tree of Life

This motif refers to trees that act as a passageway between forms of existence and those that symbolize eternal life. I include the tales of *When Your Canary Sings* (Chapter One) and *Leelinau* (Chapter Two) in this section because, although there is no Tree of Life mentioned in them, the main theme is finding eternal life or salvation in the tree. Other stories that mention the tree in a more obvious way include:

The First Dogs - Chapter Four
The Juniper Tree - Chapter Four
The Tale of Bonchevalier - Chapter Four
The Day the Sun Disappeared - Chapter Five
The Thunder Oak - Chapter Six

The Old Pine Is Blessed - Chapter Six
Legend of the True Cross - Chapter Seven
Lot and the Tree of the Cross - Chapter Seven

6. *The Earth Mother and her son, the hero or dying god*

Ancient myths about the Earth Mother and her son are abundant the world over. However, surviving fairy stories with this theme are harder to find. Much more common are stories about hero figures alone. For example, there are many long and elaborate stories told in Soviet Russia about *Ivan Sosnovich* (Chapter Five) who fits the archetypal hero profile fairly well.

I include *The Dancing Brothers* and *The Day the Sun Disappeared,* both in Chapter Five, in this category because they are stories which explain seasonal changes.

7. *Influence of Christianity*

When Christianity was introduced, the Catholic priests tried to change pagan elements in folk tales to Christian ones. They also distributed new tales of their own. Sometimes the Christian influence on a tale is slight - adding a line that says the story took place on Christmas Eve. Most often, however, the sacred character of the tree or tree spirit is changed into something to be feared or hated.

This is especially obvious when comparing the Cherokee story *Why Some Trees Are Evergreen* in Chapter One to the version *Why Evergreens Are Green* in Chapter Six. If Christian influence is not the answer, why else would the Cherokees have two stories on the same subject which portray the evergreens in such contradictory ways? The second tale is especially suspicious because, while cedar is considered sacred and is used in the older earth-oriented ceremonies of the Cherokee, cedars are described in the story as ill-willed and ungrateful. Other stories that show Christian influence include:
When Your Canary Sings - Chapter One
The Tale of Bonchevalier - Chapter Five
Silver Fir Cones - Chapter Six
The Singing Fir Tree - Chapter Six
The Thunder Oak - Chapter Six
The Old Pine Is Blessed - Chapter Six
Legend of the True Cross - Chapter Seven
Lot and the Tree of the Cross - Chapter Seven

8. *Christmas Tree stories*

This last selection is of tales specifically about the Christmas Tree.
The Thunder Oak - Chapter Six
Martin Luther and the First Christmas Tree - Chapter Seven
The Little Stranger - Chapter Seven
The Little Fir at Bethlehem - Chapter Seven
The Fir Tree - Chapter Seven

BIBLIOGRAPHY

Andersen, Hans Christian. *Fairy Tales*. Wm. Collins and World Publishing Co. Inc., 1974.

Anderson, R.B. *Norse Mythology*. Chicago: S.C. Griggs and Co., 1891.

Anesaki, Masaharu. "Japanese." *Mythology of all Races*. Vol. VIII. Boston: Marshall Jones Company, 1928.

Astley, H.J.D. *Biblical Anthropology*. London: Oxford University Press, 1929.

Belting, Natalia. *The Moon is a Crystal Ball: Unfamiliar Legends of the Stars*. New York: The Bobbs-Merrill Company, Inc., 1952.

Benedict, Ruth. *Folklore,* Reprinted from *Encyclopædia of the Social Sciences*. The Macmillan Company, 1931.

Birdwood, Sir George C.M. *SVA*. London: Philip Lee Warner, 1915.

Blaiklock, E.M. *Green Shade*. Wellington, New South Wales, New Zealand: A.H. & A.W. Reed, 1967.

Bowman, James Cloyd and Bianco, Margery. *Tales From a Finnish Tupa*. Chicago: Albert Whitman & Company, 1936.

Brundage, Burr Cartwright. *The Fifth Sun: Aztec Gods, Aztec World*. Austin: University of Texas Press, 1979.

Bulfinch's Mythology. London: Spring Books, 1964.

Bynum, David E. *The Daemon in the Wood: A Study of Oral Narrative Patterns*. Cambridge, MA: The Center for the Study of Oral Literature, Harvard University, 1978.

Campbell, Joseph. *The Mythic Image*. New Jersey: Princeton University Press, 1974.

Carpenter, Edward. *Pagan & Christian Creeds: Their Origin and Meaning*. New York: Harcourt, Brace and Howe, 1920.

Cirlot, J.E. *A Dictionary of Symbols*. New York: Philosophical Library, Inc., 1971.

Collis, John Stewart. *The Triumph of the Tree*. New York: William Sloane Associates, 1954.

Colum, Padraic. *Myths of the World*. New York: Grosset & Dunlap, 1930.

Cooper, J. C. *Illustrated Encyclopedia of Traditional Symbols*.

Crowfoot, Grace M. *From Cedar to Hyssop: A Study in the Folklore of Plants in Palestine*. London: The Sheldon Press, 1932.

Dorman, Rushton M. *The Origin of Primitive Superstitions*. Philadelphia: J.B. Lippincott & Co., 1881.

Dorson, Richard M. *Folk Legends of Japan*. Rutland, Vermont: Charles E. Tuttle, 1962.

Dorson, Richard M., ed. *Folklore and Folklife: An Introduction.* Chicago: The University of Chicago Press, 1972.

Eliade, Mircea. "Nostalgia for Paradise." *Parabola: Myth and the Quest for Meaning.* New York: The Tamarack Press, Winter 1976, pp. 6-15.

Etter, Carl. *Ainu Folklore: The Traditions and Culture of the Vanishing Aborigines of Japan.* Chicago: Wilcox and Follett Co., 1949.

Foley, Daniel J. *The Christmas Tree: An Evergreen Garland Filled With History, Folklore, Symbolism, Traditions, Legends and Stories.* New York: Chilton Company, 1960.

Frazer, Sir James George. *The Golden Bough.* Vols. I and II: *Adonis, Attis, Osiris.* New York: St. Martin's Press, 1966.

Frazer, Sir James George. *The Worship of Nature.* Vol. I. New York: The Macmillan Company, 1926.

Goldsmith, Elizabeth E. *Life Symbols.* New York: G.P. Putnam's Sons, 1928.

Green, Roger Lancelyn. *Tales the Muses Told.* New York: Henry Z. Walck, Inc., 1965.

Grimal, Pierre., ed. *Larousse World Mythology.* New York: G.P. Putnam's Sons, 1965.

Grimm's Complete Fairy Tales. New York: Nelson Doubleday, Inc.

Gupta, Sankar Sen, ed. *Tree Symbol Worship in India.* Calcutta: Indian Publications, 1965.

Hamilton, Edith. *Mythology.* New York: The New American Library, 1942.

Hasbrouck, Jean., and Mirov, Nicholas T. *The Story of Pines.* Indiana University Press, 1976.

Hastings, James, ed. *Encyclopaedia of Religion and Ethics.* Vol. XII. New York: Charles Scribner's Sons, 1908.

Heinberg, Richard. *Memories and Visions of Paradise,* Los Angeles: Jeremy Tarcher, Inc., 1989.

Holmberg, Uno. "Finno-Ugric, Siberian." *Mythology of all Races.* Vol. IV. Boston: Marshall Jones Company, 1927.

Hottes, Alfred Carl. *1001 Christmas Facts And Fancies.* New York: Dodd, Mead and Company, 1959.

Howes, Edith. *Maoriland Fairy Tales.* London: Ward, Lock & Co., Limited, 1952.

Hughes, Philip. *A History of the Church.* Vol. I. New York: Sheed & Ward, 1934.

Izett, James. *Maori Lore.* Wellington, New Zealand: John MacKay, government printer, 1904.

James, E.O. *The Tree of Life: An Archaeological Study.* Leiden: E.J. Brill, 1966.

Jones, Gertrude. *Dictionary of Mythology, Folklore and Symbols.* New York: The Scarecrow Press, Inc., 1962.

Jung, Carl G. *Man and His Symbols*. New York: Dell Publishing Co., Inc., 1964.

Kavanagh, Morgan. *Myths Traced to their Primary Source Through Language*. Vol. II. London: T.C. Newby, 1856.

Keyes, Ken, Jr. *The Hundredth Monkey*. Coos Bay, Oregon: Vision Books, No Copyright.

Krythe, Maymie R. *All About Christmas*. New York: Harper and Brothers, 1954.

Leach, Maria. *How the People Sang the Mountains Up: How and Why Stories*. New York: The Viking Press, 1967.

Leach, Maria., ed. *Standard Dictionary of Folklore, Mythology and Legend*. Funk and Wagnall Publishing Company, 1972.

Lehner, Ernst and Johanna. *Folklore and Symbolism of Flowers, Plants and Trees*. New York: Tudor Publishing Company, 1960.

Lowry, Shirley Park. *Familiar Mysteries The Truth in Myth*. New York: Oxford University Press, 1982.

MacCulloch, J.A. *The Religion of the Ancient Celts*. Edinburgh: T. & T. Clark, 1911.

MacKenzie, Donald A. *Ancient Man in Britain*. London: Blackie and Son Limited, 1922.

MacKenzie, Donald. *Myths of China and Japan*. London: The Gresham Publishing Company Ltd., 1923.

Manning-Sanders, Ruth. *A Book of Dwarfs*. New York: E.P. Dutton, 1964.

Matthiessen, Peter. "Native Earth." *Parabola Myth and the Quest for Meaning*. New York: Society for the Study of Myth and Tradition, February 1981, pp. 6-17.

Mercatante, Anthony S. *The Magic Garden The Myth and Folklore of Flowers, Plants, Trees and Herbs*. New York: Harper and Row Publishers, 1976.

Metcalfe, Edna. *The Trees of Christmas*. New York: Abingdon Press, 1969.

Muller, Fritz. *Swiss-Alpine Folk-tales*. London: Oxford University Press, 1958.

The Mythology of all Races. Vol. XII. New York: Cooper Square Publishers, Inc., 1964.

Neihardt, John G. (as told to). *Black Elk Speaks: Being the Life Story of a Holy Man of the Oglala Sioux*. Lincoln: University of Nebraska Press, 1961.

Niethammer, Carolyn. *Daughters of the Earth The Lives and Legends of American Indian Women*. New York: Macmillan Publishing Company, 1977.

Olcott, Frances Jenkins. *Good Stories for Great Holidays*. Houghton Mifflin, 1914.

Otto, Walter F. *Dionysus Myth: and Cult*. Bloomington: Indiana University Press, 1965.

Philpot, Mrs. J.H. *The Sacred Tree or The Tree in Religion and Myth*. London: Macmillan, 1897.

Porteous, Alexander. *Forest Folklore, Mythology, and Romance*. London: George Allen & Unalin Ltd., 1928.

Riordan, James. *Tales from Tartary: Russian Tales*. Vol.II. New York: The Viking Press, 1978.

Sakade, Florence. *Japanese Children's Favorite Stories*. Rutland, Vermont: Charles E. Tuttle, 1958.

Skinner, Charles M. *Myths and Legends of Flowers, Trees, Fruits, and Plants*. Philadelphia: J.B. Lippincott, 1911.

Squire, Charles. *Celtic Myth and Legend*. London: The Gresham Publishing Company Limited, 1910.

Taylor, Benjamin. *Storyology: Essays in Folklore, Sea-lore and Plant-lore*. London: Elliot Stock, 1900.

Thiselton-Dyer, T.F. *The Folklore of Plants*. London: Chatto and Windus, 1889; reissued edition, Detroit: Singing Tree Press, 1968.

Travers, P.L. "The World of the Hero." *Parabola: Myth and the Quest for Meaning*. New York: The Tamarack Press, Winter 1976, pp. 42-47.

Unkalunt, Princess Atalie. *The Earth Speaks*. New York: Fleming H. Revell, 1940.

Verrall, F.M. "British Tree Lore." *The Catholic World*, October 1938, pp. 92-98.

Walsh, William S. *Curiosities of Popular Customs*. Philadelphia: J.B. Lippincott, 1898.

Weiser, Francis X. *The Christmas Book*. New York: Harcourt, Brace and Company, 1952.

Weiser, Francis X. *The Holyday Book*. New York: Harcourt, Brace and Company, Inc.,1956.

Wentz, W.Y. Evans. *The Fairy-Faith in Celtic Countries*. Atlantic Highlands, New Jersey: Humanities Press, 1911.

Wilson, Robert Anton. "The New Age Interview: Rupert Sheldrake." *New Age Journal*. Brighton, MA: Rising Star Associates, Ltd., February 1984, pp. 43-45, 84-87.

Whittick, Arnold. *Symbols, Signs and Their Meaning*. London: Leonard Hill, 1960.

INDEX